For original illustrations
by Chase Stone visit
GodsofThrones.com

GODS OF THRONES

A PILGRIM'S GUIDE TO THE
RELIGIONS OF ICE AND FIRE

VOL.2

A.RON HUBBARD   ANTHONY LE DONNE

"*Gods of Thrones Vol. 2* masterfully plumbs the depths of the ancient mythologies and premodern rituals, beliefs, and practices that inspire the lore of the old gods and the theology of the new—and everything in between. Inherently accessible and compulsively readable, Hubbard and Le Donne offer up a new and fascinating lens through which to view the competing and overlapping belief systems that undergird Westeros—and threaten its demise."

— JANA MATHEWS, PHD
Professor of Medieval Literature
Rollins College

"A skillfull analysis full of deep insight on both religion and the mega-hit Game of Thrones. This adroitly written second volume continues to explore the myriad dimensions of faith and the world of Westeros in a truly entertaining and engaging way. A mind needs books—especially ones like this—just as a sword needs a whetstone."

— JOSEPH M. VALENZANO III, PHD
Professor and Chair of Communication
University of Dayton

"*Gods of Thrones* does what few books on the 'religion and pop culture' scene do -- not suck. The authors demonstrate their love of the story and provoke us to deeper engagement. *Gods of Thrones* is an invitation to take the religious landscape of Martin's world seriously, recognizing its complexity and depth, and at the same time provide scholarly insights from across the our own history of the divine. If you like to ask humanity's oldest campfire questions and love yourself some GOT then get your life a win and read this book."

— TRIPP FULLER
Author, podcaster, and founder of Homebrewed Christianity

Printed in the United States of America

First Printing, 2019

Original illustrations by Chase Stone.
Graphic design by Steve Gentile.

GODS

OF

THRONES

True hope is swift, and flies with swallows' wings;
Kings it makes gods, and meaner creatures kings.

—WILLIAM SHAKESPEARE

Volume 2

PREFACE

I N OUR FIRST VOLUME, O siblings of septology, we began our pilgrimage along the sacred paths of fire and ice. We traversed the cruel North, land of frost giants, tree gods, and spirit animals. We paid homage to the old and new gods. We sojourned with Ned, Catelyn, and their children. We sailed to Essos with Tyrion to escape divine judgment and toured the fiery temple of Asshai.

In this second part of our journey we're ready to open diplomatic channels with the Night's Watch, the Faceless Men, the dragonlords, and (though diplomacy is rarely fruitful) the Dothraki. The watchful eyes of the Drowned God and the Great Shepherd will be upon us as we revisit a few of our favorite characters. We will explore the deep-seated duality of Jon Snow and the unlikely fortune of Samwell Tarly. Our journey will take us into Tyrion's devotion to a dragonish cult of personality and Arya's stubbornly wolfish identity. We will dive deep near the Iron Islands where krakens roam and then sail easterly through the Stepstones. You might even see a mischievous merling off the starboard bow... keep an eye on *that* one.

Touring George R. R. Martin's thoughtscape is a bit like time travel. His fictional cultures remind us of our own legacies. Martin loves the nooks and crannies of history and leaves symbolic Easter eggs for his readers. He drops hints when he describes the Wall, dragonlords, Jaqen's coin, direwolves, etc. If we want to interpret these symbols we will need a refresher course on Hadrian's

Wall, Chinese dragon gods, death coins, and Irish-Catholic werewolf lore. These episodes from our own history are not pretty and in some cases altogether R-rated.

The lion's share of this book is about the in-world settings, plots, and characters of the *Song* series and its HBO adaptation. We explore the religions of this world alongside the many cultures and traditions that parallel our own ancient and premodern histories.

This book exists because we've fallen in love with Martin's key players and we wanted a reason to spend more time with them. If you're like us, you've got your favorites and you've got characters you love to hate-watch. We want justice for Arya's lost childhood and worry about what she will become in the process. We'd like to imagine that we're half as witty as Lady Olenna or half as sly as Littlefinger. We desperately want Dany to win the game of thrones even though it may well drive her mad. And if you've read *Gods of Thrones, vol. 1*, you already know that we're dreaming of a post-Iron Throne springtime.

That said, this book isn't just fanboy celebration (although we often lapse to our default). Martin's characters and plotlines flourish in ethical ambiguity and are thus open to critique. This book will touch the fraught topics of colonialism, masculinity, and racism. These criticisms are usually found in our "Bird's-Eye View" sections that conclude each chapter.

Finally, yes, there are spoilers ahead. Enter at your own risk. We wrote this book before the airing of the final season of the HBO series and before the publication of *The Winds of Winter*. Keep this in mind if you're reading this book after 2019. It is possible that some of the fan theories featured in these pages will seem even more absurd in your present than they do in ours. Our philosophy on the matter is that even the most absurd theories remain evergreen and will be incorporated into the 2175 reboots. We just hope that by then the AI-GRRM-collective construct will have published *A Dream of Spring.*

Contents

Here Be Dragons

THE DARK HEART OF THE DRAGON CULT

8

Birds can fly but will fall at the hunter's arrow. Fish can swim but will be hooked by the fisherman. Beasts can run but will drop into people's nets and traps. There is only one thing that is out of man's reach. That's the legendary dragon. A dragon can fly into the sky, ride on clouds, dive into the ocean. A dragon is powerful yet so intangible to us. Lao Tzu is a dragon, and I'll never understand him.

—CONFUCIUS

Distinctive Elements

- ✤ divinely represented royalty
- ✤ ruling-class ideology
- ✤ occasional facility with dragon magic

Key Adherents

- ✤ Aegon Targaryen
- ✤ Tyrion Lannister
- ✤ Khaleesi (you know, *Khaleesi*)

TRAVEL GUIDE

WESTEROS HAS DESIGNATED the air over King's Landing as a no-fly zone. But visitors traveling by way of the kingsroad, rigged sail, or Gendry-powered boats are welcome to tour the capitol. Visitors to the Dragonpit ruins will want to arrive early as it has recently increased in popularity. We recommend arriving before the hour of the nightingale to avoid crowds. While the official Iron Throne press release states otherwise, dragons are back in fashion and have the smallfolk buzzing about Targaryen celebrities.

There are few architectural feats that live up to their reputation when seen in person, but the Dragonpit of King's Landing does not disappoint. Standing atop the Hill of Rhaenys, the domed arena once housed the dragons that conquered the Seven Kingdoms. The dome was large and strong enough to hold Balerion the Black Dread. The arena had iron doors wide enough for thirty knights to ride through side by side. Even though it's massive dome is partially collapsed, many visitors express an almost spiritual sense of awe and dread. Standing in the spot that once contained creatures of godlike power and scale is a humbling experience for mere mortals.

Local rumors suggest that three live dragons may be returning to the capitol. While this may explain the no-fly zone proclamation, the threat level has not risen above Falkor-level and it hasn't been at Smaug-level for centuries.[1]

Here Be Dragons: The Dark Heart of the Dragon Cult

1. Dragon threat levels ranked by most dangerous (10) to least (1):
   10. Nidhogg
   9. Typhon
   8. Bahamut
   7. Ancalagon the Black
   6. Smaug
   5. Balerion the Black Dread
   4. Beowulf's Bane
   3. Hungarian Horntail
   2. Falkor the Luck Dragon
   1. Pete's Dragon

DEEP DIVE:
DRAGONS JUST GONNA DRAGON

THERE MUST ALWAYS be a Stark in Winterfell; at least this is what they say north of the Neck. It is a lovely notion, comforting to followers of the "old ways" (although opinions differ among the Boltons). It is especially comforting to Starks who benefit from hereditary titles and the mythos of Winterfell. Starks ruling the North is just the way it's supposed to be. This tradition is what the ancient Egyptians would call *ma'at*.

The term can be translated as "order" but *ma'at* is a special kind of order. *Ma'at* is the natural and social order mediated by the pharaoh that promotes truth, justice,

and harmony. In other words, all the things that Superman brings to Metropolis. But pharaohs were far more
powerful than Kryptonians. Without *ma'at*—which only
the pharaoh could provide—political success and fertil-
ity were impossible. It would be like if Superman fought
for truth, justice, the American way, while also magically
governing all sex, food, courtrooms, and the military.[2]

It is perhaps the best bit of political propaganda
ever devised: *if the pharaoh is in power, all is right in
the world; if the pharaoh is*—gods forbid!—*cut off, the
world will fall into total chaos.* In the Stark version of this
myth, the blood of the "First Men" justifies their right of
succession. But it's more than just bloodlines, it's *ma'at*:
a Stark governing the North is what tells us everything
is going to be okay.

Of course, there is no dynasty that better embodies *ma'at* than the Targaryens. Not only do these blue-
blooded autocrats think they're born to rule, they parallel
Egyptian royalty in several ways. Both the pharaohs and
the Targaryens rule through the authority of historic
bloodlines. Both marry brothers to sisters. And both
maintain royal power backed by supernatural power. In
the case of the pharaohs, the ruler embodies the solar
god (pharaoh is son of Ra). In the case of the Targaryens,
the ruler is the embodiment of a dragon (usually named
for a Valyrian deity). In both cases, there is order in the
land as long as the ruler maintains a spiritual connection
to the supernatural power behind the throne.

To call this ideology "religious" isn't quite right
(the concept of religion hadn't been invented yet). But
the idea of *ma'at* plants the ideological seeds for many
future religions. At this point in Egyptian history, we're
not really talking about religion; this is mythological language to fortify political power. In the case of

*Deep Dive: Dragons Just
Gonna Dragon*

2. Lest you think that this sounds
like an improvement, we have it
on good authority that Superman
is both strictly missionary and a
gluten-free vegan. Which … there's
nothing wrong with that. But it's not
for *everybody*, you know?

3. Famously, the Greeks borrowed many divine categories from Egypt; Rome borrowed the same categories from the Greeks.

4. Archmaester Gerold writes that before Aegon Targaryen conquered Westeros, "there was hardly a time when two or three of these kingdoms were not at war with one another" (*World*, "The Conquest").

the pharaoh, he wasn't "religious" any more than you could say that the Greek or Roman gods were pious.[3] The Egyptian gods were not necessarily all-knowing or benevolent. Rather, they were archetypal and powerful in superhuman ways. In Westeros, the power behind Targaryen rule is dragon magic. Dragons (functioning as demigods in this story) share a spiritual connection with dragonlords and give them the power to bring order to "seven quarrelsome kingdoms."[4] The fact that they name their dragons after Valyrian gods is telling. For the conquering Targaryens, mythology is primarily a political tool.

Targaryens are adept at using religion as a means to legitimize their supernatural power. This explains why the first Targaryens in Westeros (arriving before the Doom of Valyria) built a sept for the Seven-Faced God at their Dragonstone castle. While the true power behind their conquest was dragon magic, the veneer of religion was somewhat arbitrary and was easily exploited. In reality, they functioned as a dragon cult. This cult was imbued with superhuman power and fortified with mythology.

5. See, for example, the work of Clifford Geertz (1926–2006).

Excursus: Isfet

Scholars of religion have varying (and evolving) definitions for religion. One possible definition is that *religion is a system of symbols that attempts to manage chaos.*[5] While this is a modern definition, the problem of chaos is explored in several ancient myths that predate modern religion. In Egyptian mythology, the word for chaos is *isfet*. It can also mean injustice or deceit. *Isfet* (chaos) is destroyed by creating space for *ma'at* (order) through the divine power of the pharaoh. According to one text,

> Ra has placed the king
> On the earth of the living
> For all eternity;
> Judging men, satisfying gods,
> Bringing order *(ma'at)* into being,
> annihilating chaos *(isfet)*.
> He gives divine offerings to the gods
> And funerary offerings to the dead.

But annihilating *isfet* isn't easy, Jimmy. It's like holding back the waves of the sea to create more solid ground. Indeed, deep water—with its unpredictable fluidity and violence—becomes a metaphor for chaos. Not only is deep water dangerous to navigate, it is the territory of monsters.[6] For example, Apep is the god/monster of chaos who brought *isfet* and attacked *ma'at*. He is depicted as a giant serpent. Apep is a precursor to dragon mythology for future storytellers.

Deep Dive: Dragons Just Gonna Dragon

6.   The Bible probably borrows a couple of sea monsters from Egyptian stories. The Book of Job mentions "Behemoth" and "Leviathan" which are similar to how the Egyptians thought of the hippopotamus and crocodile.

Before Aegon, Visenya, and Rhaenys took to the sky to conquer the Seven Kingdoms, they paused to pray. The Targaryen siblings conspired with their bannermen, prepared for conquest, then "visited the castle sept to pray to the Seven of Westeros as well." According to Archmaester Gerold, Aegon "had never before been accounted as a pious man" (*World*, "The Conquest"). This detail about his character makes him similar to his ancestors who "regarded all faiths as equally false, believing themselves to be more powerful than any god or goddess. They looked upon priests and temples as relics of a more primitive time, though useful for placating

'slaves, savages, and the poor' with promises of a better life to come" (*World*, "Norvos").

The hint about Aegon's lack of piety is almost a throwaway detail in Gerold's account. The line isn't in parentheses, but it might as well be. Gerold is far more interested in telling us about Aegon's sisters who became his wives (more on incest below; we know you can't wait). Yandel writes that Aegon was a man of "vision and determination," but leaves his purpose and motives vague (*World*, "Aegon I"). Martin's history suggests that Aegon was spurred to war by an insult from Argilac, the Storm King. More likely, however, is that Aegon's conflict with the Stormlands sparked a conquest that he had been planning all along.[7] Whatever the case, Aegon the Conqueror (also called "the Dragon") does not seem to be driven by devotion to the Seven.[8] He did, however, form a strong alliance with the High Septon at the Starry Sept early in his conquest.

In truth, we are not given much insight about Aegon's reason for conquest. We know that Aegon and his sisters were politically savvy and powerful enough to hammer lesser kings into their lords. We know that Visenya was a serious, well-trained warrior. Her austere and unforgiving personality is detailed by Gerold. We know that Rhaenys was a free spirit, interested in performance arts and entertaining guests. She was known for her love of flying with her dragons. Aegon's motives, however, are unknown. Why does he want to rule the Seven Kingdoms? What makes him think he has the right to rule anything?[9]

Our best guess—and you can decide how educated it seems—is that dragonlords seek to rule because that is what dragonlords do. As Gyldayn says, "Who can know the heart of a dragon?" (*The Princess and the Queen*).

Here Be Dragons: The Dark Heart of the Dragon Cult

7. According to the account in *Fire and Blood*, Aegon has been planning his conquest long before as evidenced by the early crafting his famous table (built as a model of Westeros and meant for devising wartime strategies). Gyldayn writes, "Plainly, Aegon's interest in Westeros long predated the events that drove him to war" ("Aegon's Conquest").

8. Martin was asked, "Did Aegon Targaryen convert to the Faith as a political maneuver?" His reply was simply, "Yes." See the So Spake Martin Archives, July 2008.

9. *Fire and Blood* is over 700 pages long. George, you couldn't include a couple lines about Aegon's motivation?

Perhaps it is not so much a question of motive; it is more a matter of nature. *Dragons just gonna dragon, yo.*

Those who place their faith in the power of dragon magic know that monsters act like monsters. Even if well managed, a monster like Balerion the Black Dread was not a pet.[10] Balerion's shadow was the size of a small town and his teeth were like swords (*Clash* 12, Daenerys 1). He was large enough to eat an aurochs whole and breathed black flame.

And, if the legends are true, he once bested Willem Dafoe in a staring contest.[11] One can hardly blame Balerion for roosting at the pinnacle of the food chain.

But what does it say of a Targaryen prince who believes himself to be a dragon in human form? Or what does it say of a queen who believes herself to have dragon's blood? Metaphorical or otherwise, if you call yourself a dragon this says something about your character. Some might say that Targaryens who boast the "Blood of the Dragon" are claiming to stand at the top of the political food chain.

This is the dark heart of the dragon cult: those who claim to have dragon's blood are essentially claiming to be a ruling class. Gerold tells us first and foremost that the "Targaryens were of pure Valyrian blood, dragonlords of ancient lineage." He continues,

> Aegon had two trueborn siblings; an elder sister, Visenya, and a younger sister, Rhaenys. It had long been the custom amongst the dragonlords of Valyria to wed brother to sister, to keep the bloodlines pure, but Aegon took both his sisters to bride. . . All three siblings had shown themselves to be

Deep Dive: Dragons Just Gonna Dragon

10. *Zaldrizes buzdari iksos daor.*

11. It was a best two out of three contest but Dafoe was a much younger man.

23

dragonlords before they wed (World, "The Conquest").

Here Be Dragons: The Dark Heart of the Dragon Cult

Keeping "bloodlines pure" is, of course, the concern of many royal families (both real and fictional). It is also the foundation of most ruling-class ideologies. The marriage of brother and sister is an extreme example of blood purity (e.g. the practice of ruling-class incest of Ancient Egypt). More usual was the practice of "endogamy." Endogamy is the practice of marriage within one's own tribe. This might include incest but more often paired cousins or more distant relatives. The underlying concern is often to keep the "bloodlines pure."

For the Targaryens of Westeros, the hope was to avoid diluting the blood of Old Valyria. Presumably, there was something about this bloodline that facilitated dragon magic with great efficiency. So Gerold's comment tells us two things: blood purity (1) kept dragonlords in the family, and (2) kept Targaryens in power.

Targaryen incest also explains something important about their drive to conquer. The early Westrosi Targaryens prioritized blood purity so much that they shunned marriage arrangements outside the family. While other houses were building political power through marriage alliances, Aegon, Visenya, and Rhaenys had to find another way to climb the political ladder. Aegon refused marriage proposals from the Stormlands and the Vale that might have won him land peacefully. His commitment to blood purity, coupled with his ruling-class aspirations, made military conquest almost inevitable.

As the Targaryens became more entrenched in Westeros, they began to wed their lesser sons and daughters to other great houses.[12] But Targaryen brother and

12. For example, Queen Alysanne Targaryen arranged marriages with other houses, often aggressively. This excerpt from *Fire and Blood* illustrates her agenda: "When Her Grace suggested that she would be pleased to help arrange marriages for his sons to the daughters of great southern lords, Lord [Alaric] Stark refused brusquely. 'We keep the old gods in the North,' he told the queen. 'When my boys take a wife, they will wed before a heart tree, not in some southron sept.' . . . The lords of the south honored the old gods as well as the new, she told Lord Alaric; most every castle that she knew had a godswood as well as a sept. And there were still certain houses that had never accepted the Seven, no more than the northmen had . . . Even a lord as stern and flinty as Alaric Stark found himself helpless before Queen Alysanne's stubborn charm." Pre-publication excerpt provided by George R. R. Martin, "A Fire & Blood Excerpt Just For You!" Not a Blog, September 27, 2018.

sister continued to marry on occasion and were willing to fight wars with the Faith Militant over the issue (*Fire and Blood,* "Prince into King").

Deep Dive: Dragons Just Gonna Dragon

Excursus: Dragon Magic

In Martin's world, dragons aren't just large, dangerous reptiles. Dragons are physical beasts animated by (or bred and empowered with) magic. For example, Balerion was known to breathe black fire hot enough to melt stone (*World,* "Conquest"). This is a clear literary hint that dragon fire derives from some kind of supernatural source. The showrunners build on this with blue fire breathed from a zombie dragon.[13] At the macro level, Martin's entire ecosystem intermingles with magic. He sets the stage with a supernatural cycle of seasons. Not only are dragons infused with magic, they seem to supercharge the magic of Martin's world in several ways. Examples include the pyromancers and Warlocks of Qarth; both groups seem to have been magically strengthened by the birth of Dany's dragons. It is also possible that the ability to resurrect the dead is made possible by the return of dragon magic. Both Thoros and Melisandre seem surprised by the power of their rituals.

---

13. Eat your heart out, Rick Grimes.

At this point, if you're like us, you're thinking: *We get it, George. The Blue Lagoon was your favorite movie! Can we please dispense with the incest plotlines?* But if we dig deeper into our own mythologies—from which George borrows—we see that the ancient world was rife with ruling class endogamy and incest. Moreover, humans have been making the gods into their own image for centuries. Stories of brothers wedding sisters can be found in Chinese, Norse, Egyptian, Greek, and Roman mythologies.

Jupiter and Juno get Hitched: This fresco (1st cent.) depicts Jupiter wedding his sister Juno. Photograph by Marie-Lan Nguyen; courtesy of Wikimedia Commons.

In the case of Ancient Egypt, the gods were famous for this. Shu (god of air) and Tefnut (goddess of rain) are siblings who hook up to produce two children. These two are the brother-sister combination of Geb (god of

26

Earth) and Nut (goddess of sky[14]). Geb and Nut do the tower-of-joy dance and produce four children who pair off in the same way.

One explanation for this divine pattern is that it reflects the practice of the Egyptian royalty (e.g. the parents of Tutankhamen).[15] Not only did the pharaohs often pair brothers and sisters, they claimed to represent divinity on Earth. This is a close parallel to the way Targaryans think about their own connections to dragons. In short, both Egyptian and Targaryen royalty claim to be superhuman, perhaps even a superior species. Most importantly, gods are only accountable to the gods. Put another way, dragons follow the rules of dragons. The morality of common folk simply does not apply.

Martin isn't simply drawing from his own dark fantasies. He's borrowing from a common myth that ruling-class people use to justify their behavior. It is the myth that special people deserve to be exempt from the moral restrictions of the unwashed masses. As the Targaryens became normalized within the Faith of the Seven, the religion minted a new doctrine just to accommodate them: the Doctrine of Exceptionalism (*Fire and Blood,* "A Time of Testing"). In short, the new doctrine simply stated that the traditional rules about incest didn't apply to the ruling class. *The Seven made both the lion and the bull, yet the gods do not expect the lion to eat grass.* This isn't just the dark fantasy of Targaryen lore; it is the dark reality of ruling class ideology. Because the other side of that doctrinal coin is the unspoken: *be content with your grass, lest the lion eats you.*

This brings us to an uncomfortable question about the character of our favorite Breaker of Chains: Daenarys Targaryen. When Dany hatches her dragons, she enacts something like a human sacrifice.[16] This act makes Dany

14. And orgasms, *hey oh!*

Deep Dive: Dragons Just Gonna Dragon

15. Katie Moisse, "Tutankhamen's Familial DNA Tells Tale of Boy Pharaoh's Disease and Incest," Scientific American, Feb. 16, 2010.

16. Martin has been overly coy with his non-answers to the question of dragon hatching and human sacrifice. Martin was asked in an interview, "The birth of a dragon seems to be connected to fire and death. Does birthing a dragon require a human sacrifice?" He answered, "Interesting notion. I mean there are clues in the books, uh, so, you know. I think I'm going to dodge that one right now." We think that some non-answers are sufficiently revealing. See "George R. R. Martin on the World of Ice and Fire," youtube.com; Feb. 28, 2018.

the mother of dragons and begins her quest for the Iron Throne. Why is the fan base so quick to forgive Dany for burning Mirri Maz Duur at the stake like a medieval witch? Do we believe that the usual rules of morality do not apply to her? Does her ruling class blood justify her fire-and-blood path to power? To the point, Dany's burn-them-all tendencies are a key theme of season seven. Both Varys and Tyrion worry that she might go all mass-murdery like her father.

What makes Dany's burning of Mirri, Randyll, or Dickon (no giggling) Tarly any different than what Melisandre did to Guncer Sunglass? The most obvious difference is that Melisandre is a religious zealot who murders fools to please her Lord. Dany, on the other hand, burns fools who stand in the way of her conquest. Does the blood of Old Valyria justify psychopathic behavior?

Finally, the fact that she has teamed up with Melisandre in season seven reminds us that dragonlords are known to use a veneer of religion as a political tool. Dany seems to like the idea of being the embodiment of a religious prophecy, and we won't be surprised to see her embrace the prophets of Asshai. But don't be fooled. She is completely devoted to herself.

She tells Jon that her "faith" has sustained her in exile. "Faith. Not in any god, not in myths and legends. In myself. In Daenerys Targaryen." (Referring to oneself in the third person is some Lex Luthor-level villainy.) "I was born to rule the Seven Kingdoms and I will" (S07E03, "The Queen's Justice"). The concerns of Tyrion and Varys are not unwarranted.

HISTORICAL BACKDROP:
SONS OF DRAGONS

MARTIN'S INTEREST IN dragons is shaped in large part by European legends. In this world, dragons are creatures of magic and fire. They are "fire made flesh" (*Clash* 27, Daenerys II). The connection to fire recalls Beowulf's dragon in particular. But dragon lore is common in many ancient and medieval cultures. Dragons (great, serpentine creatures) feature in Egyptian, Babylonian, Jewish, Greek, Russian, and Japanese legends.

Japanese Dragon: Japanese artist Katsushika Hokusai (1760–1849) is perhaps best known for his woodblock and print work. In this case, his painting of a dragon is reminiscent of the Ukiyo-e style that was popular from 17th-19th centuries. Courtesy of Wikimedia Commons.

17. Most of this section is owed to
John Thorbjarnarson and Xiaoming
Wang, *The Chinese Alligator: Ecology,*
Behavior, Conservation, and Culture
(Baltimore: The Johns Hopkins
University Press, 2010).

18. Thorbjarnarson and Wang,
Alligator, 61. *T'o* is notoriously
difficult to translate. It seems to apply
to any number of large water lizards
in ancient texts.

In Martin's world, there are a few unmistakable parallels to Chinese dragon mythology.[17] Chinese dragon mythology probably grows out of alligator lore. The Chinese logogram *T'o* is sometimes interpreted as alligator and sometimes as earth dragon.[18] This association is key to understanding their place in mythology and religion. In the Tang, Qing, and Han dynasties, dragons were treated as rain gods that governed the weather. They were thought to reside below water (being of the same family as alligators). In the work of Confucius, dragons tend to show up prior to or just after rainfall.

During times of drought, farmers performed rituals to get the attention of sleeping dragons. Some of these rituals—like submerging a tiger skull in the river—were supposed to scare the beasts out of the water and into the sky. According to tradition, the simple act of a dragon moving from water to sky would bring rainfall. Dragons were sort of like agents of the water cycle before modern science had a better word for it. Other rituals—like ritually beating a small lizard to death with bamboo—would get the dragon's attention in the same way a sacrificial offering was meant to work. In northern China, regular prayer was performed to dragons before the rainy season to ensure good crops.

The first ritual demonstrates the place that dragons and tigers occupied in mythology. The tiger symbolized drought, while the dragon symbolized rain. From this perspective—yin (dragon) and yang (tiger)—dragons were necessary and positive. These were not the fell beasts of European lore or the sociopathic greed-monsters of Inkling imagination; rather dragons were rain deities, bringing fortune with them. It is important to keep in mind that such deities were not—like western minds associate with divinity—all-knowing or all-powerful. Dragons were divine in the sense that they were mythological beasts with powers that could sometimes be manipulated by humans. Only, it didn't always go well for the humans.

Chinese emperors have a long history of using dragons as sigils. In the same way that the dragon is able to ascend from water to heaven, the emperor also ascends to heaven. The association was meant to reinforce the great power of royalty: they had god-like powers. Bang Liu (206–195 BCE) was called the dragon's "Seed" meaning that his father was a literal dragon. As the first emperor of the Western Han Dynasty, Bang Liu's legend cemented the ruling class as sons of dragons (i.e. they were sons of the gods, comparative to Egyptian Pharaohs).

Emperor Chengzu clothed in Dragon Robes: This silk scroll depicts Emperor Chengzu of the Ming Dynasty wearing dragon emblems on his robes. Courtesy of Wikimedia commons.

31

This backdrop shows a few obvious parallels to Targaryen mythos and few obvious differences. The most glaring difference is that Martin's dragons are fire-breathing, warmongering gluttons. They may represent fortune (for those who can point them in the right direction and say *dracarys*) but they also represent mass destruction. They are not, in other words, like rainfall in a drought (which benefits everyone). In this way, Martin's dragons are decidedly influenced by European legend. Also, Martin's dragons don't sleep underwater and get spooked by tiger skulls. That said, the parallels are too intriguing to dismiss.

1. The Targaryens use dragons as their sigils.

2. Dragons are associated with the Old Valyrian gods (e.g. Balerion, Meraxes, Vhagar, and Syrax are all dragons named after gods).

3. The Targaryens believe themselves to be related by blood to dragons.

4. Daenerys (a.k.a. "Stormborn") is born during a famously rainy night.

Could it be that Martin was influenced in some way by Chinese dragon mythology?[19] And if so, consider this: the main benefit of Chinese dragons is to bring positive balance to the weather. Could it be that Martin's dragons are meant to restore balance to the imbalanced seasons of Westeros?[20] Maybe the Westerosi farmers who don't get marshmallowed by Dany will benefit from spring showers after the Others are defeated.

19. Probably.

20. Possibly.

Dragon Temple, Dashkasan (Iran): Outside a series of caves in Iran is a temple constructed by Chinese craftsmen. This ornate dragon carving inspired the common name for the site, "The Dragon Temple," also known as "Dragon Stone." Courtesy of Wikimedia Commons.

CHARACTER STUDY: TYRION

LOOK, WE DON'T know if Tyrion is a secret Targaryen. In volume one, we gave a few good reasons to consider this fan theory. But reasonable people can disagree. What is clear—what we will argue with great argumentative arguing—is that Martin has something big planned for Tyrion. Consider the evidence:

1. Early in the story, Tyrion is foreshadowed as a big deal—perhaps in the sense of royalty, but at least in the sense of Burgundy. This happens for the first time after his famous exchange with Jon Snow, "All dwarfs may be bastards, yet not all bastards need be dwarfs." Martin then uses a literal shadow to foreshadow: "When he opened the door, the light from within threw his shadow clear across the yard, and

for just a moment Tyrion Lannister stood tall as a king" (*Game* 5, Jon I).

2. Maester Aemon says that Tyrion is a "giant come among us, here at the end of the world." Tyrion protests but Aemon doubles down on the compliment (*Game* 21, Tyrion III).

3. Moqorro (priest of R'hllor) tells Tyrion that he's a small man with a big shadow (*Dance* 33, Tyrion VIII).

These three literary omens interest us because each has a dragon hiding in plain sight. Also, having three points is good for arguments when you're feeling especially argumentative. Jon Snow—as we all now know—is a secret Targaryen. Aemon was a secret Targ before being a secret Targ was cool (*Game* 60, Jon VIII). And while Moqorro is not a dragon, he gives insight into Tyrion's character in a conversation about dragons and while holding a dragon headed staff. Martin is famous for leaving breadcrumbs like this for his readers.

Again, we're not trying to confirm any fan theories at this point. As far as we *know*, Tyrion is a lion, not a dragon. But whatever we make of his rumored parentage, Martin has set up Tyrion to be a dragon cult convert.

Early in his story, we find Tyrion reading a book about the properties of dragon bone. He admits to having a morbid fascination with dragons since his youth (*Game* 13, Tyrion II). Indeed, Tyrion is probably the most well-read expert on dragon lore beyond the walls of the Citadel. His famous line "I drink and I know things" is said in a conversation about the history of dragons. Benioff and Weiss add to this backstory. According to the show, Tyrion wanted a pet dragon as a boy and cried himself to sleep when he learned that dragons were extinct (S06E02, "Home").

Sigurd slays Fáfnir: In this scene from Norse mythology, Fáfnir (formerly a dwarf) has become a dragon by the curse of Andvari's gold. He is eventually slain by Sigurd who drinks Fáfnir's dragon blood and cooks his heart. In some versions of the myth, Fáfnir was not a dwarf but a giant. Artist: Arthur Rackham (1911); Courtesy of Wikimedia Commons.

Season six also affords Tyrion his most clear statement of devotion. He confesses to Dany that he's always been a cynic. He was never able to believe in gods, family, or even himself. "I said 'no thank you' to belief and yet here I am. I believe in you" (S06E10, "The Winds of Winter").

Even if we focus only on book canon, Tyrion's endgame is clear. His identity crisis will land him squarely in the service of Daenerys Targaryen, the dragon queen. He will renounce all previous service to the gods, lords, and clans of Westeros. And he will, indubitably, ride a dragon into battle thus becoming a giant warrior—nay, *a god*—among men! Either that, or Tyrion will be murdered for no apparent reason.

FAN-THEORY FUN: DAENERYS IS NISSA NISSA REBORN

AFTER READING OUR deep-dive take on Dany, perhaps you're ready to conspire against her and plot her untimely demise. Martin has said that he envisions a "bittersweet" ending to *A Song of Ice and Fire*. What would be more bittersweet than Jon being forced to kill Dany in order to save the day? This theory builds from the assumption that Jon "secret Targ" Snow will fulfill a prophecy and defeat the Others with a magic sword that can only be created by stabbing Dany in the heart.[21] You might want to skip this part; it's going to get weird.

In a legend told by Lord of Light loonies, the White Walkers (lead by the "Great Other") have threatened the world before. A warrior named Azor Ahai was able to hold back the darkness using a magic sword. Azor Ahai didn't know about ladies in lakes who hand out swords upon request. So he tried to forge it himself, working on it for thirty days and tempering it in water. No luck. Mr. Ahai tried again and worked on it for fifty days and tempered it by plunging it into the heart of a lion. No luck. He tried for a third time, smithing the sword for one hundred days. This time—and the rationale here is a

21. While early seeds of this theory were planted by Ser Grimes on "A Forum of Ice and Fire" (December 9, 2012), fully fleshed out treatments are owed to redditors Lord_Bronn (2013) and MrVanillaIceтCube (2016). Also, we would be remiss not to mention ASOIAF FAQ at angelfire. com in 2004. Among several possibilities, "Maester Luwin" suggested that Dany is Azor Ahai and Drogo is Nissa Nissa. It's worth noting that Dany has, in fact, tried to forge her fiery weapons (dragons) twice before her ultimate success. In her third and final attempt, she brings her dragons to life upon the pyre of her spouse.

bit vague—he knew that he needed to temper the sword with heart of his wife, Nissa Nissa. In other words, the process required a human sacrifice. She apparently had Jesus in her heart because the sword got super salvific. Her soul fused within the sword like L3-37 uploaded into the *Millennium Falcon*.[22] Once Azor Ahai had forged the sword (called Lightbringer), he was able to save the world from perpetual cold, darkness, and giant spiders (totally worth it).

Fan-Theory Fun: Daenerys is Nissa Nissa Reborn

22. In some legends, such as Japanese and Norse mythologies, famous swords are possessed by or guided by disembodied souls.

Wolf Attacking a Wyvern: Outside the cathedral of Saint Vigilius (Trent, Italy) is this carving of a wolf and wyvern fighting (a wyvern is a winged dragon with only two legs). Photography by Matteo Ianeselli. Courtesy of Wikimedia Commons.

According to Melisandre and Thoros, Azor Ahai will return to save the day again (*Clash* 10, Davos I; *Storm* 54, *Davos* V; Dance 10, Jon III). Fans who truck with this theory hypothesize that Jon Snow will have some reason to sacrifice Dany on his way to defeating the Night King. In this way, he will reenact the legend and turn into the supercharged savior of Westeros. This assumes that (1) Melisandre will finally predict something correctly, (2) Jon Snow will indeed be the reincarnation of Azor Ahai, (3) Jon will literally reenact the whole wife-murder ritual, and (4) Dany will need to play the part of the Nissa Nissa in this scenario.

With so many moving parts, it isn't surprising that there are several variations of this theory. Perhaps there will be a literal sword. Perhaps Dany *is* the metaphorical sword. Perhaps Dany is the "princess that was promised" and Jon is Azor Ahai reborn (this assumes that these are two different figures). Perhaps Jon's betrayal of Ygritte proves what he is willing to do and foreshadows a second betrayal. Or perhaps Jon himself is a metaphorical Lightbringer, and he tempered himself with Ygritte's betrayal and there is no more need for a second.

While we can't disprove this theory, we have mixed feelings about it. Do we really want to root for a dude who has just ritually sacrificed his lover? Also, it would be disappointing if Dany only exists to birth dragons and support Jon's heroism. One of the best qualities of Martin's world is the stage it provides for compelling female characters. An event like Dany reenacting the Nissa-Nissa ritual might potentially undermine that legacy.

BIRD'S-EYE VIEW:
SILVER SAVIOR?

THE FINAL EPISODE of HBO's season three is titled "Mhysa." The reason for this title becomes obvious in the final scene. It shows the freed slaves of Yunkai hailing Dany as "mhysa," meaning *mother*. And if the matriarchal overtones aren't enough to persuade you, the showrunners depict Dany surrounded by her adoring masses while her children (dragons) fly through the air. Even if Mirri Maz Duur is right and her womb never quickens, she is fast becoming the most important matriarch in the world. Considering that Dany began her journey as a child bride who was essentially sold into marriage against her will, this is a breathtaking plateau for her character.

But has Dany's ascension come on the shoulders of the nameless, brown masses? And if so, isn't this just another example of the white savior fantasy? We're not the first to ask these questions. When "Mhysa" first aired on June 9, 2013, it was seen by over 5.4 million U.S. viewers. Inevitably, some of those viewers were going to notice the awkward image of a white teenager being worshipped by thousands of brown bodies.[23] To many of those viewers the problem is obvious. But to others, some background on the white savior story is needed. Sociologist Matthew W. Hughey explains:

> *A White Savior film is often based on some supposedly true story. Second, it features a nonwhite group or person who experiences conflict and struggle with others that is particularly dangerous or threatening to their life and livelihood. Third, a White person (the savior) enters the milieu and through their sacrifices, as a teacher, mentor, lawyer, military hero, aspiring writer, or wannabe Native American warrior, is able to physically save—or at least morally redeem—the person or community of folks of color, by the film's end.*[24]

Bird's-Eye View (Part 1): Silver Savior?

23. Recently Martin was asked about this scene. He explained that the scene was shot in Morocco and therefore it was Moroccans who answered the casting call as extras. "George R.R. Martin on Racism and Sexism Accusations against Game of Thrones," youtube.com, Jan 15, 2019.

24. Matthew W. Hughey, "the whiteness of oscar night," *Contexts*, 2015.

So is "Mhysa" an example of a White Savior fantasy? At first glance, the answer is no. Hughey's first criterion is that the fantasy is based on a supposedly true story and *Game of Thrones* is not. But we'll circle back to this in a bit.

Next, do the brown people in Dany's story experience life-threatening struggle? The Yunkai slaves certainly do. Missandei's livelihood is not exactly threatened but she's certainly enslaved and exploited before Dany comes along. The Dothraki do, but they—like Walter White—*are the danger.* The Unsullied are reared for the sole purpose of deadly conflict. Yet let's not forget that they are literally slaves. So the answer is complicated, but for a few of these, we have a definite yes.

Finally, does Dany enter the struggle with her unique talents to save or redeem the brown masses? This is an emphatic *yes.* Dany sees herself as a savior and attempts to *dracarys* her way toward Essos liberation. This is, in fact, is her primary plotline for season three. It is worth pointing out that Dany's dragonlord ancestors popularized the institution of slavery in Essos (*World*, "Valyria's Children"). She is only able to act heroically because of the damage done by her forefathers.

Because the second two criteria are yes and yes, let's take a closer look at the Hughey's primary observation: the trope "is often based on some supposedly true story." He lists several examples that include *Glory, Dangerous Minds,* and *The Blind Side.* But Hughey is aware that historical fictions and fantasy/sci-fi films feature white saviors too, giving examples such as *The Last Samurai* and *Avatar.*[25] Sometimes the story doesn't have to purport to *be true;* it can simply *ring true.* In other words, it uses brown (and sometimes blue) bodies to bring "authenticity" to the fiction. We are now firmly

25. Hughey does not list C-3PO's ascension to divinity in *Return of the Jedi* as an example. We will note, however, that C-3PO—while not white—is certainly blonde.

in *Game of Thrones* territory. This world is compelling because it seems authentically medieval.[26]

The trouble with using racial categories to bring authenticity to fantasy is that western audiences tend to have a selective memory when it comes to history. Let's remember that European history was shaped from the borders by many non-white rulers including Attila the Hun, Genghis Khan, and Mansa Musa. Musa (of Mali), for example, was well-known throughout Europe for his wealth and architectural projects. He may well be the wealthiest person in history.

Bird's-Eye View (Part 1): Silver Savior?

26. Which, by the way, is the primary objection to the employment of more actors of color. Those who have a vanilla view of medieval Europe tend to defend the overuse of white actors. In other words, they want *Game of Thrones* to feel racially "authentic."

Mansa Musa I of Mali: This 1375 (CE) depiction of Mansa Musa is preserved in the Catalan Atlas. Courtesy of Wikimedia Commons.

In terms of influence from within, Christendom was dominated for centuries by Constantinople, hub of the Byzantine Empire (western Asia). More to the point, Islam expanded to several European cities and maintained a steady presence in Spain for centuries (711–1492). The modern myth of a lily-white Europe is just that: a modern myth. Even if we grant that medieval

England was predominantly pale and expect a mirror image in Westeros, there is no historical reason to project whiteness onto the Targaryens, who are from Essos.

Maybe the best argument for more complexity in *Game of Thrones* comes from the blog of Chinedu Hemingways. "Let's set aside historical plausibility for a sec and focus on the fact that the show isn't rooted in anything real. It's a fantasy for Christ's sake! You've got dragons and zombies but can't think up a black-led kingdom?"[27] Chinedu suggests an empire modeled after ancient Egypt. More to the point, the Targaryens could have easily been cast as Egyptians and it would have been no less authentic.[28]

27. Chinedu Hemingways, "Where Are All The Black People in Game of Thrones?" OkayAfrica.com, July 2017.

28. Chinedu offers the following disclaimer: "In Game of Thrones, white people build empires . . . show great valor, strategy and more all while protecting their humanity from the greatest threat ever imaginable to man—zombies and incest (yea we ain't about that life, leave us out of that)."

Here Be Dragons:
The Dark Heart of the
Dragon Cult

Excursus: Casting Color

One of the repeated slams of HBO's adaptation has been its failure to include more non-white characters in key roles. Or as the pilot episode of Netflix's *Dear White People* observes, "That shit with dragons set in the world where no one's black except the slaves?" The accusation isn't exactly true but characters like Salladhor Saan and Xaro Xhoan Daxos are few and far between. The sentiment has its finger on a problem that is true of most fantasy literature: *fictionalizations of the medieval past tend toward Eurocentric whiteness.*

Saan is played by the British-Tanzanian actor, Lucian Msamati. Daxos is played by the British-Nigerian actor, Nonso Anozie. In the books, neither character is from the Summer Isles and therefore would not be considered black to modern eyes. Martin originally imagined Saan as Lyseni and Daxos as Qartheen. So the show-runners are at least nodding to diversity. But they also removed two important (book-only) characters entirely: Moqorro and Brown Ben Plumm. *The second of these examples has "Brown" right in his name!* Moreover, Plumm claims to have a Valyrian branch in his family tree. Martin's world could have included dark-skinned, royal lineage if the showrunners had been willing. We would have liked to see him played by Lavell Crawford ("Huell" from *Breaking Bad*).

No doubt, part of the "blame" goes to Martin for making the Targaryens blue-blooded whites. They literally have violet eyes and silver hair in the books. That said, Benioff and Weiss are complicit too. While they have often deviated from Martin's book-described character appearances (often just because a literal depiction of a book character would be patently ridiculous—*we're looking at you, Daario*[29]), they chose to maintain the image of a silver-haired Dany surrounded by a worshiping, brown underclass.

We will end this section with two questions built from Chinedu's point, "the concept of race as a human differentiator didn't exist until about the 16th century." He is right. The consensus among scholars of ethnic studies is that the concept of race is a modern construct. The ancient world had caste systems, political bloodlines, peasants, and underclasses. But these were rarely (if ever) determined by skin color.[30] Benjamin Isaac summarizes that "the concept of race as such is merely theoretical, since it is a quasi-biological construct invented to establish a hierarchy of human groups and to delineate differences between them. . ."[31]

Bird's-Eye View (Part 1): Silver Savior?

29. Book Daario is described as keeping his beard cut in three prongs, all dyed blue. His curly hair is dyed blue, no doubt to match his eyes and colorful garments. His mustache is painted gold, underlining his large, curving nose. His smile reveals a golden tooth. His personal arms bear hilts that are a matched pair of naked women fashioned in gold (*Storm* 42, Daenerys IV). Of all these outlandish details only the "trucker mud flap" hilts were included in his screen portrayal.

30. More to the point, skin color is only one kind of phenotype (physiological characteristic) that seems to have become important for power dynamics in the modern world.

31. In reality, the modern period simply reinforced the stereotypes using pseudoscience (such as phrenology). From this perspective, *racism* existed long before our modern conception of race was invented. Isaac writes, "The designation *'race'* in the sense of subspecies cannot be applied by definition to language groups (the Aryan race), national groups (the English race), religious groups (the Christian or Jewish race), groups with one or more physical features in common, such as skin color, or the entire species of humans (the human race): such usages are biologically and scientifically meaningless" (*The Invention of Racism in Classical Antiquity* [Princeton: Princeton University Press, 2004], 33).

Here Be Dragons:
The Dark Heart of the
Dragon Cult

True to form, we never hear race discussed in Martin's world. Some credit is due to Martin and the showrunners for not projecting a modern construct onto an ancient setting. On the other hand, the audience of *Game of Thrones* lives in a political world built on racial dynamics. It is impossible for modern eyes not to see race. And if so, shouldn't Martin, Benioff, and Weiss have been better aware of their audience? Also, if they had been better aware, what should they have done differently?

We imagine that there is no simple answer to these questions. But they are questions worth asking nonetheless.

Night Gathers

WARRIOR MONKS, WARGS AND, LIKE, A WIZARD

9

The last brick goes in then, as he sings goodbye at the end of the song. That is the completion of the Wall. It's been being built in my case since the end of the Second World War, or in anybody else's case, whenever they care to think about it, if they feel isolated or alienated from other people at all.

—ROGER WATERS

Distinctive Elements
- life-long monasticism
- militaristic
- democratic
- *corn! corn!*

Key Adherents
- Jon Snow
- Samwell Tarly
- a wretched hive of scum and villainy

WANDERING CROW'S GUIDE

THE NIGHT'S WATCH wants *you!* They are looking for a few good crows. When you've had enough fantasy football and Facebook rants, join up with the most elite fighting force north of Mole's Town. Come to the True North and live a life of adventure. The black brotherhood will give you a higher calling, a civic duty, and a perfectly legal means to murder giants and gingers.

The Night's Watch is the oldest military branch in Westeros and the most honorable. Learn a trade as an apprentice with the builders. Get a leg up on the service industry with the stewards. If you're among the ever-stalwart elite, you can see the world with the rangers. Assuming that you don't die in the process, you can always count on one square meal a day of reheated turnips (voted best edible root vegetable by the *Castle Black Gazette*).

Some recruits may qualify for the craven-reversal program. This includes (but not limited to) night hikes along the 700-foot high ice wall, repeated beatings while balled up in the fetal position, and sub-zero marches that make you want to become one with the tundra. *Semper frigus!*

DEEP DIVE: THE REALMS OF MEN

DEFINING RELIGION—*WHAT IT is, how it's invented, what purpose it serves*—is tricky and you'll get different fancy words from different fancy folks. Previously we pointed to Durkheim, who was French-level fancy. He said that religion is a higher level of human consciousness that organizes society. We've also tipped our caps to Geertz, who said that religion is an attempt to hold back chaos. (Chaos is the opposite of fancy.) If you talk to fancy-pants people of faith, they might say that religion is an attempt to live toward a higher, supernatural reality.

By all three of these definitions, the Night's Watch is a deeply religious institution. It organizes men of all backgrounds toward a higher purpose. In fact, it creates a "sworn brotherhood" in the same way that a monastery does. It organizes its communal life around the myths, traditions, and rules of the Wall much like an island people might live next to a volcano god: there is no part of life untouched by its looming reality. Most importantly, the Night's Watch holds back the darkness that exists beyond the Wall. This line of their oath is telling: *the shield that guards the realms of men.* It's an age-old oath repeated before the brothers and before the gods.

For modern sociologists, a communal oath to hold back darkness sounds religious. To medieval ears, the oath would sound like a monastic vow. David Benioff explains that the Night's Watch is "like a cross between an ancient monastic order and a special forces brigade."[32]

What's that you say? You think that militaristic monks are a contradiction in terms? Go watch *The Last Jedi.* They exist and they drink Thala-siren milk straight from weird, walrus crotch-teats. Not convinced? Consider the Teutonic Knights.

Their full name was "Order of Brothers of the German House of Saint Mary in Jerusalem." This brotherhood is best known for shepherding European pilgrims into Jerusalem circa 12th century. The pilgrimage was a popular Christian trek at the time and became a preoccupation of Christianity. But this fascination for the "Holy Land" often became a motive for militant crusades and the Teutonic Knights were no exception.

Like the Night's Watch, these knights were divided into different occupations. Some were monastic, some preserved a line of crusader castles, and some ranged broadly committing acts of chivalrous thuggery. Of course, they believed they had a noble cause. The Teutonic Knights saw themselves as an "order"—in other words, they were organized around a set of rules. They were also an order in another way: they were a defense against the chaos-causing infidels.[33]

This isn't a bad way to think about the Night's Watch. From one perspective, the brothers are warrior

Deep Dive:
The Realms of Men

32. "The Night's Watch by George R. R. Martin," youtube.com, May 21, 2016.

33. An idealized remembrance of the Teutonic Knights featured in German nationalism before and during the rise of Nazi ideology. Heinrich Himmler promoted the SS as a modern version of these knights. Eventually Hitler banned actual membership of the order in 1938, fearing the return of a Catholic military branch. This, by the way, is the same reason that King Maegor defeated and outlawed the Faith Militant in Martin's world.

monks with a noble calling. They have a chaste lifestyle in service to the realm. From another, they are "crows" that range to into enemy territory reinforcing the divide created by the Wall. In sum, what the Wall does supernaturally, the brotherhood enacts socially.

Tannhäuser in Teutonic Surcoat: Tannhäuser (13th century) was a German poet who is remembered in legend as a knight. He is depicted here in a white surcoat with the cruciform symbol of the Teutonic Knights. Courtesy of Wikimedia commons.

PARALLELS BETWEEN THE NIGHT'S WATCH AND MEDIEVAL MONASTIC ORDERS

Monastic Orders	Night's Watch
period of initiation before full membership	period of initiation before oath
commitment to rule before God	commitment to oath before the gods
communal living	communal living
exclusively male or female communities	exclusively male community
initiates called "brothers" or "sisters"	initiates called "brothers"
vow of celibacy	oath of no wife and no children
vow of poverty	oath against holding lands or crowns

Parallels between the Night's Watch and Medieval Monastic Orders

The Wall was originally meant to divide human territory from the territory of the Others (see "Crueler Gods" in vol. 1). But with so few sightings of an actual snark or grumkin, the Wall was repurposed to keep out a different sort of chaos. It is a crucial bit of propaganda, therefore, that the tribes beyond the Wall are labeled "wildlings."

The Free Folk are considered *wild* because of their savagery. (Like most propaganda, it contains a kernel of

34. For example, it is true—albeit politicized—that all baby rattlesnakes become venomous by suckling the teats of Chuck Norris.

truth.[34]) This allows the Night's Watch to maintain the myth that organized society exists only on the Westerosi side of the Wall. In short, devotion to the Night's Watch is driven as much by fear as it is by loyalty or belief in the supernatural. These elements are seeds for misgivings and, in some cases, justification for institutional violence.

The ingredients used for religion building are the same ingredients used for tribe building. It is a social formula that creates a sense of community (with all of the benefits of intimacy and belonging) and a sense of insiders vs. outsiders (fortified by xenophobia). We see both sides of this coin in the Night's Watch. From one view, it brings together highborn and baseborn into a democratic fraternity. It creates a sense of family for disowned boys and criminals in need of a second chance. But its dark side is in full view as well: it creates a literal barrier between their society and the savages beyond the Haunted Forrest. The fact that the Wall is supernatural and ancient justifies their ritual violence against the creatures of chaos.

Given the ancient and supernatural barrier between the Night's Watch and the Free Folk, it would take something extraordinary to assuage their mutual fear and hatred. It would take an even deeper magic to bring the groups together. In *A Song of Ice and Fire*, the would-be bridge builder is a warg.

Excursus: What is a Warg?

Martin seems to have borrowed the term warg from Tolkien. The original R. R. coined the term after *vargr*, the Norse word for wolf. In Tolkien's world, a warg is an intelligent, albeit evil, wolf. Sometimes aligned with goblins, they are large enough to serve as their steeds. They do not transform into humans, nor are they mentally controlled by them. Tolkien's *Silmarillion* does, however, feature one human character named Beren who transforms (for a short time) into a great wolf. Perhaps then, Martin merges these stories as he imagines Westerosi wargs.

Parallels between the Night's Watch and Medieval Monastic Orders

Jon Snow's devotion and loyalty to the Night's Watch is both militaristic and monastic. This is to say that Jon imagines himself as a ranger (a soldier that ranges into enemy territory) and a celibate devotee (in lifelong service to his calling). Jon has knit this identity into his psyche at a young age. During his awkward existence under Catelyn's roof, the idea of the Night's Watch provided a glimmer of hope for Jon. Otherwise he was just Ned Stark's bastard and always would be. As much as he loved his father and brothers at Winterfell, his uncle Benjen represented a new life. Jon had been preparing himself for the sworn brotherhood all of his life.

At the same time, Jon betrays a deep-seated duality. He is both Ned's son and not. Even before we know that he is both Snow and Targaryen, we know that he is first and foremost *not a Stark*. But Jon's loyalty to House Stark is central to his identity. When Robb marches south, Jon is torn by his brotherly love for Robb and his vows to the sworn brotherhood. Jon is a boy of both tribes.

Jon, in the end, remains loyal to the Night's Watch. But his social status is awkward at the Wall too. His oxymoronic nickname "Lord Snow" shows Jon's duality in a nutshell. Jon was born with all of the benefits of a highborn son of Winterfell. That is, he has all the benefits except for the all-important family name.

His duality runs even deeper. Jon isn't just a bridge between tribes; he is a bridge between human and wolf. He occupies (even if only in his dreams) two different bodies, one civil and one feral. He's got *Duran Duran* desires and Warren Zevon zoomorphy.

One of the first things we know about direwolves is that they are naturally at home north of the Wall (*Game* 1, Bran 1). Jon's spiritual connection to Ghost tells us that he is, deep down, a creature of the True North. Had Jon grown up north of the Wall, he might have learned what it meant to be a warg. Instead he finds himself misplaced and alienated from his own fundamental identity. As Robert Louis Stevenson wrote, our "man is not truly one, but truly two."[35]

Jon Snow is therefore the perfect person to become both a sworn brother and a wildling. Or, put another way, he is both a crow and free. Martin foreshadows Jon's affinity for the True North when Jon says his vows. Had he—like most of his fellow novices—followed the new gods, Jon would have repeated his vows before Septon Celladar. But having the blood of the First Men in his veins, Jon must go beyond the Wall to say his vows before a Heart Tree (*Game* 48, Jon 6). His devotion to the old gods gives him another early point of connection with the cultures beyond the Wall.

His time with Ygritte is a crucible for his loyalty. His duality beyond the Wall involves both his devotion to the Night's Watch (something he always wanted) and his love for her (something he never thought he'd have). He's both a literal and metaphorical skinchanger: some-one who is human and wild at the same time.

Night Gathers:
Warrior Monks, Wargs
and, like, a Wizard

35. Robert Louis Stevenson, *The Strange Case of Dr. Jekyll and Mr. Hyde* (New York: Charles Scribner's Sons, 1886), 106. The fuller quote by Stevenson is too good not to include: "With every day, and from both sides of my intelligence, the moral and the intellectual, I thus drew steadily nearer to that truth, by whose partial discovery I have been doomed to such a dreadful shipwreck: that man is not truly one, but truly two."

In the end, it takes someone with the sensibilities of a warg to reform (or destroy) the Night's Watch. For millennia, the sworn brotherhood had all the zeal of religious gatekeepers who defended traditional barriers as much as they defended against evil. But in electing Jon as Lord Commander, they open the door to social chaos. And chaos is the antithesis to both religious and tribal devotion.

Parallels between the Night's Watch and Medieval Monastic Orders

Gargoyle of a Werewolf: This werewolf styled gargoyle can be seen from Denfert-Rochereau Blvd. in Cognac, France. Photograph by Père Igor; courtesy of Wikimedia Commons.

HISTORICAL BACKDROP: WEREWOLVES IN RELIGIOUS THOUGHT

THE ANCIENT GREEKS told many stories about humans turning into animals. Wolves, in particular, were likely candidates. One possible explanation is the psychiatric condition known as lycanthropy (*lykanthropos* means "wolf-man" in Greek). In this condition, the afflicted person believes that he or she sometimes transforms into a wolf. Perhaps some of the early stories about werewolves stemmed from this psychosis.[36]

In one story, the king of Arkadia offered a child sacrifice to Zeus. His name was Lycaon—roughly translated to "Wolfie"—which should have given the king some clue about his fate. Stories vary about whether Lycaon sacrificed his son or grandson. In either case, Zeus was displeased and turned the king into a wolf. This, of course, happened on Mount Lykaion. In other stories, the mountain attracted priests of Zeus who performed sacrificial rituals. One of the rituals involved a feast of various meats mixed with human flesh. Any person who ate the human flesh became a wolf. The person could return to human form provided he avoided eating human flesh for nine years. *Thus pulling off the best practical joke ever.*

In some medieval Jewish literature, it is assumed that humans occasionally transform into wolves. In these cases, we're not dealing with full moon-fueled beasts. These medieval writers imagined that some dudes just completely wolf-out and remained wolfed-out indefinitely. In many cases, these werewolves keep their human minds but have difficulty communicating with their former human friends.[37]

In one short passage in *Sefer Hasidim*, Judah the Pious is working through the logical problems of transformation. Specifically, this rabbi considers the story from Genesis about the serpent that, as a result of God's curse, lost its humanoid form and transformed into a legless creature (Genesis 3). Judah supposes that such a transformation is only possible if there is some continuity in form. He solves the problem by observing that both humans and snakes have round eyes. The same logic goes

36. We have absolutely no evidence of this. We just needed an excuse to show off our formidable lycanthropy knowledge.

37. Much of this section borrows from David I. Shyovitz, *A Remembrance of His Wonders: Nature and the Supernatural in Medieval Ashkenaz* (Philadelphia: University of Pennsylvania Press, 2018), 138-143.

for werewolves, says Judah. After all, everyone knows that werewolves, when in lupine state, maintain human-oid eyes. Were-science. You just can't argue with it.

Another example comes from the French rabbi, Ephraim ben Samson. In the 12th century, werewolf lore was as popular as it had ever been in Europe. Tales of barons and knights who devolved into wolves flourished like *Twilight* prequels. While Christian authors were borrowing from Ovid's *Metamorphoses*, Jewish authors drew from the Bible. For example, Genesis 49:27 says metaphorically, "Benjamin is a ravenous wolf." But in werewolf-crazy France, the metaphor was too intriguing to resist. According to rabbi Samson, this verse meant that Benjamin was, in fact, a werewolf.[38]

We don't witness the height of wolfmania until we see Catholic disputes in their full glory. Some argued that it was heretical to believe in werewolf superstition. Some argued that the appearance of werewolves represented demonic tricks. But some, like Gerald of Wales, attempted to baptize werewolf lore into Catholic theology in his *Topographia Hibernica*. Gerald relayed a story that was told to him by a cleric from Ulster (Ireland).

This local priest had encountered a wolf that spoke to him. The wolf claimed to be a human and (most importantly) a Catholic. Unfortunately, he and his wife had both been cursed and turned into wolves. The priest, as anyone in this situation would, quizzed the werewolf on Catholic doctrine until he was convinced that the beast was indeed telling the truth.

Once convinced, the wolf explained that his wife was close to death and required last rites. So the priest walked with the wolf to the ailing she-wolf. He was unsure if it was proper to administer communion to Catholics in lupine form. The werewolf begged the

Historical Backdrop: Werewolves in Religious Thought

38. It is impossible to tell how widespread the belief in werewolves was in medieval Jewish life. It is possible that only a few folks actually believed in these stories. Maybe a majority of French rabbis rejected the existence of werewolves. But where's the fun in that?

priest to do it but the priest was still reluctant. Finally, in a last-ditch effort to prove his wife's humanity, the werewolf tore the skin from her to reveal an old woman beneath the she-wolf veneer. The priest administered a last communion for the woman. Before she died, the werewolf replaced his wife's wolf skin.

The story created a stir among other clerics who debated whether or not the priest acted according to right doctrine. Gerald was unable to answer whether werewolves were really humans. But he used the occasion to explain the higher mysteries of the Incarnation and the Eucharist.[39] The Incarnation teaches that God transformed into human form in the person of Jesus. The Eucharist transforms bread and wine into the body and blood of Jesus. *Look,* he argued, *if you're going to believe in divine transformations, you shouldn't be too quick to dismiss werewolves.*

CHARACTER STUDY: SAMWELL

S AM IS BRAGGING to Gilly about his knowledge of the Nightfort. By reputation, it's equal parts haunted house and military fortress. It is abandoned, in ruins, and rat infested. The Nightfort is the perfect setting for Old Nan's ghost stories. But that's not what interests Sam. Sam knows—or so he boasts—where to find the Black Gate, which will take them through the Wall and safely out of White Walker territory. The Black Gate has not been used in centuries but Sam has read about it in a very old book.

Gilly asks, "You know all that by staring at marks on paper?" He says yes. Then she gives Sam the gift he's always wanted. Not only is Gilly impressed with his bookish charm, she looks at him in awe and says,

"You're, like, a wizard" (show only; S03E09, "The Rains of Castamere").

Such a phrase, when uttered with just the right inflection, by just the right wildling wench, is nerd catnip. The look of bliss on Sam's face tells the whole story; he's basking in the afterglow of a Ferengi eargasm.[40]

Gilly's reaction to arcane book knowledge captures the mystique of writ in ancient cultures. When 99% of commoners cannot read a book, those who can read possess real power. In most ancient cultures, some commoners could write their names or read a shopping list. But the ability to read an old book and learn something long forgotten was rare even for social elites. If the book in question was sacred, a book expert became a powerbroker of the supernatural.

Character Study: Samwell

40. Technically speaking, the practice of oo-mox would not violate the vows of the Night's Watch.

Excursus: What is a Wizard?

The distinction between a general facility with knowledge (i.e. wisdom) and expertise in magic didn't exist in premodern times like it does today. This can be seen in many cultures that employ shamans as arbiters of wisdom. The category "wizard" is a window into the early 15th century. The root of the word in Middle English was *wys*, which simply means "wise." It didn't take long, however, for the word to evolve. By the 1550s, *wys* took on a sense related to occult knowledge. It is no coincidence that this era is on the cusp of modernity (as we now divide these stages of history).

Night Gathers:
Warrior Monks, Wargs
and, like, a Wizard

As they approach the Wall, Gilly voices the medieval view that books are something close to magic. Considering her upbringing, it's likely that she's never met anyone with Sam's education. It's also possible that Sam, through his research in the Castle Black library, knows more than any living person about the Wall's supernatural nooks and crannies.

Surely, there are maesters at the Citadel that have studied longer. And there is "Marwyn the Mage" who has traveled abroad studying the higher mysteries. But most maesters are skeptics of magic (or simply oppose it) and few have visited the unique holdings of the Castle Black library. All this is to say that Gilly is right: Samwell Tarly is, like, a wizard.

Instead of a magic wand, Sam wields the magical properties of dragonglass. And instead of incantations, he's memorized the vows of the Night's Watch. But make no mistake, he's well on his way to becoming "Samwell the Wise." Or, in the words of Pyp, "Sam, Sam, Sam the wizard, Sam the wonder, Sam Sam the marvel man!" (*Storm* 79, Jon xii). Of course, the title means a lot more when it is bestowed by Gilly. In her one-line affirmation of his wizardry, Sam receives admiration from his crush and realizes that a life-long dream has come true. Because Sam, of course, has always wanted to be a wizard.

Long before Sam finds dragonglass or learns the words to open the Black Gate, he confesses his wizard dreams to Jon Snow. Jon has learned that he's been chosen to be a steward of the Night's Watch, rather than a ranger. Jon laments that he always wanted to be a ranger. In an effort to console his friend, Sam replies, "I always wanted to be a wizard" (show only; S01E07, "You Win or You Die").

This is Sam expressing his absurd existence as the eldest son of House Tarly. His father wanted a warrior and a hunter. Sam's father wanted a stereotypical male or nothing at all. This is no overstatement. According to Sam, Randyll Tarly intended to murder Sam or send him the Night's Watch. Randyll would rather kill his son, cover up the deed, and live with the lie rather than have a coward inherent his lands and title. *Always wanted to be a wizard* might be Sam's way of saying that he wasn't the son his father wanted. Never did he realistically think that he might become an actual wizard one day. But in Gilly's eyes, he is every bit that wizard of his youthful daydreams.

Character Study: Samwell

Here we have something truly remarkable in Martin's multiverse multiverse: *a character who dreams of becoming something and achieves it.*

FAN THEORY FUN: ARE ALL STARK CHILDREN WARGS?

EVERYONE KNOWS THAT Bran Stark is a skinchanger. And by "everyone" we mean the eleven people who know what a skinchanger is. This means he is capable of transferring his consciousness into another body. (Notable hosts are Summer when he's hunting and Hodor when he's hodoring). In *Song,* a "warg" is a skinchanger who can project into a wolf. Bran, therefore, is both skinchanger and warg. He's also a greenseer, capable of prophetic dreams and leaving his body to observe other times and places.

If we haven't lost you already in the tall grass of geekdom, you may want to know that most of Rickard Stark's known grandchildren[41] have shown at least a minimal level of wargism.[42] Martin has long main-

41. Saying "grandchildren of Rickard Stark" is an effort to be precise, because as nerds we're natural pedants. Saying "Eddard Stark's children" would exclude Jon Snow, who we now know is the child of Rhaegar Targaryen and Lyanna Stark. We'll refer to them as the Stark children going forward.

42. No, this is not a real word.

43. So Spake Martin Archive,
Feb. 1, 2001

44. *Author morghulis.*

45. Still not a word.

tained that he intended this from the beginning. The following exchange with an astute reader provides the strongest evidence, "Are all the Stark children wargs/skin changers with their wolves?" Martin responded, "To a greater or lesser degree, yes, but the amount of control varies widely."[43]

Nevertheless, authorial intent or retrospective can never tell us the whole story. Many literary theorists argue that a piece of writing enjoys a second life beyond authorial intent wherein the author yields authority.[44] Furthermore, a subset of these academics are in no way egomaniacal and self-serving. Fans who believe that the meaning of Martin's work extends beyond his jurisdiction may well be interested to know that most of the Stark children have demonstrated a capacity for wargism[45] beginning in the earliest novels. We'll consider them in order of most evidence to least.

Bran: In both the show and the book series, Bran commandeers his wolf as well as fellow human Hodor. The ethical questions related to Bran's forcible control of Hodor's body are controversial (he may well be the Zebediah Killgrave of greenseers). But because Bran's status as a warg is obvious and because we devote an entire chapter to him at the end of this book, we'll move on.

Jon: Unfortunately, nearly all of the evidence for Jon being a warg comes from the books and is largely subtext or altogether absent in the show. For example, when ranging beyond the Wall with Qhorin Halfhand, Jon is asleep and Ghost is miles away hunting. In this context, Jon dreams of spying on the massing wildling army in the Frost Fangs. When he sheepishly recounts his dream to Qhorin and his men—all experienced rangers and familiar with the legends of skinchanging from their dealings with Wildlings—they immediately recognize that Jon has accidentally warged into Ghost (*Clash* 53, Jon VII).

After the battle at Castle Black, Jon begins to feel an overwhelming hunger and need to hunt, to "kill and fill his belly with fresh meat and hot dark blood" which he finds confusing (viz. warg puberty; *à la* Teen Wolf). Without seeing or hearing the wolf, he realizes Ghost has returned after being separated since the Qhorin adventure. Jon calls out to Ghost, who immediately appears and rejoins his side. Even after a long separation and being out of practice, Jon is able to intuitively connect to Ghost (*Storm* 79, Jon XII).

Fan Theory Fun: Are all Stark Children Wargs?

The renegade wildling skinchanger, Varamyr, recognizes Jon as a powerful warg on sight, stating "one skinchanger can always sense another." He also notes, "the gift was strong in Snow, but the youth was untaught, still fighting his nature when he should have gloried in it" (*Dance*, Prologue).

Arya: The youngest Lady Stark presents an interesting example. Arya is parted from Nymeria early on in the series after Nym bites the royal arsehole, Prince Joffrey. You'd expect that not being able to bond and practice subconscious warging would be a hindrance to her innate abilities, but in the books there is ample evidence of Arya skinchanging.

After escaping Harrenhal, Arya dreams of being hunted down by the Bloody Mummers. She sees Nymeria (or through Nym's eyes) following them and tearing them to pieces, allowing her escape. We later find out these dream events actually happened, and the fearsome direwolf managed to kill at least four of the Mummers, ripping one's arm off entirely (let the wookiee win).

Arya manages to see a wolf pack in the distance and childishly howls at them. The largest stops, faces

46. In a bittersweet detail, Bran
does the same thing a book earlier
(*Clash* 4, Bran 1) with Summer and
Shaggydog.

her, and howls back, causing her to shiver.[46] We later find
out that Nymeria is leading a massive wolf pack in the
riverlands and is making sport of the Frey and Bolton
forces stationed there (*Storm* 3, Arya 1).

Later, Arya has another dream from Nymeria's
perspective where the wolf discovers the body of Catelyn Stark among the bodies floating down the war-torn
Trident River. She drags the corpse out with her jaws
(*Storm* 65, Arya XII). The Brotherhood without Banners
discovers the body of Mama Stark and gives new life to
the terrifying Lady Stoneheart.

Finally, when Arya is blinded as part of her Faceless
Men training, she sometimes views scenes "through
the slitted yellow eyes of the tomcat purring in her lap,"
gathering information to give to her assassin trainers
(*Dance* 45, The Blind Girl). As all feline lovers know,
getting anything whatsoever useful out of a cat requires
uncanny powers. *It is known.*

As is typical, the show does not contain any of
these details. We do, however, get a post-book glimpse
of Arya's brief reunion with Nymeria. Arya is elated, and
is excited to take Nym back with her to Winterfell. But
the she-wolf rejects Arya's offer and returns to the wild.
This rejection parallels Arya's rejection of her parents'
plans to establish her as a polite, predictable, and noble
lady (S07E02, "Stormborn").

Robb: In the books as well as on screen, we hear of
pro-Lannister propaganda that paints Robb as a monster
that transforms into a wolf at will. Talisa also scares two
Lannister squires with this rumor (show only; S05E03,
"Kissed by Fire"). While he can't transform into a wolf,
the rumor is rooted in Robb's spiritual connection
to Grey Wind.

The element of surprise is a key reason for Robb's early campaign success. All passages from the riverlands to Casterly Rock are guarded by the Golden Tooth, a watchtower that commands the hill road entering the westerlands. As such, Tywin Lannister is confident that Robb cannot move his army west without being detected. However, according to the books, Grey Wind shows Robb a "goat track" through the mountains just wide enough for a horse and rider to pass single file (*Clash* 39, Catelyn v). Many fans surmise that Robb saw this passage in a wolf dream while Grey Wind was on the hunt. It could be that his warg-scouting, combined with some other clever spycraft, enables Robb to humiliate the much more experienced Lannister commanders in battle after battle.

We also know that Robb's wife, Jeyne (Talisa in the show) worries that Robb spends an inordinate amount of time staring at his battle plans late at night, refusing food or drink, completely unresponsive to her attempts to rouse him or draw his attention (*Storm* 20, Catelyn III). This is consistent with the behavior of someone who is having a wolf dream (even if semiconscious).

In a morbid but bloody awesome detail, the books reveal Robb's last words are "Grey Wind" (*Storm* 51, Catelyn VII), which mirrors Jon's last words after his mutiny at Castle Black: "Ghost." We find out later that Grey Wind managed to escape his confinement at the Red Wedding and goes on a rampage (*Storm*, Epilogue) killing four Frey wolfhounds and tearing the arm off of their kennel master. The suggestion is that Robb wargs one last time into Grey Wind to extract a measure of fury and revenge against his betrayers.

Rickon: On both page and screen, Rickon's status as a warg is only subtext. The books tell us that Rickon is

Fan Theory Fun: Are all Stark Children Wargs?

"wild" and that Shaggy is as "wild as Rickon." The small boy and wolf pup visit the crypts of Winterfell alone on multiple occasions, without any torches or other ways to guide them. Rickon also has the same prophetic dream of Ned visiting the crypts of Winterfell that Bran receives, which foreshadows Lord Stark's death at King's Landing (*Game* 66, Bran VII).

Empathy with his wolf pup and greendreams were among Bran's early manifestations of his gifts. If both Bran and Rickon have the same prophetic dream, does this suggest that Rickon also has greensight? Could Rickon have developed this gift too with time and training? Though if we were to offer some advice to book-Rickon, it would be to forget the wolf stuff and practice running away from things in a zig-zag pattern.

Sansa: As you can see with the previous examples, all of the Stark children who demonstrate their gifts do so initially through their relationships with their direwolves. Sansa betrays her sister to protect her betrothed, the aforementioned Prince A-hole, which results in the execution of her direwolf pup, Lady (*Game* 16, Eddard III; S01E02, "The Kingsroad"). Since this happens so early on in the story, it seems reasonable that Sansa would have much more difficulty exploring her gifts with such a handicap.

Some fans have suggested that Sansa did in fact charm a canine. One reader suggests that Sansa's vivid dreams of Sandor "the Hound" Clegane are telling.[47] Perhaps the strange affinity that Sandor Clegane felt towards her in her captivity at King's Landing is an example of untrained and instinctive use of very low-level warging. We remain skeptical, however, as any sort of manipulation of an intelligent person would seem to preclude the idea of "untrained" and "low level." It's also

47. Redditor "Oxymephorous" writes, "Sansa does have some pretty intense dreams, which feature prominently in her dialogues, and dreaming seems to be the preliminary step in warging. Quite a few of her dreams involve Sandor Clegane; it's been theorized that he replaced Lady as her protector when the direwolf died. Paraphrasing the quote from King Robert: 'A direwolf's no pet; get her a *dog* and she'll be happier for it.'" Reddit.com, June 20, 2012.

possible that Sansa's early learning of political manipulation via Littlefinger will be strengthened by this latent ability, and perhaps this will be explored in *Winds* or *Dream*. However, this does not appear to be the case in the show, where Littlefinger is brought down by a combination of Bran's greenseeing, Sansa's political savvy, and Arya's skill with a blade (S07E07, "The Dragon and the Wolf").

In conclusion, it certainly seems that in the books, Martin followed through with his intention to make all of the Stark children have these gifts of the old gods, with Sansa being an easy-to-explain exception. In adapting the story, the showrunners have chosen to underplay and/or omit entirely these character traits.

BIRD'S-EYE VIEW: HADRIAN'S WALL

IN 1981, GEORGE Martin was visiting a friend in England. Like many tourists who travel northward, he stopped in Northumberland, an area once known as the home of the Humbers (or "Umbers"). The county is named for the lands north of the River Humber (actually an estuary) and marks the northernmost lands of England.[48] There he visited Hadrian's Wall and set the foundation for what would become Westeros. Hadrian's Wall—now home to several archeological sites—once marked the end of the Roman Empire. Martin recalls:

> *I stood up there and I tried to imagine what it was like to be a Roman legionary, standing on this wall, looking at these distant hills. It was a very profound feeling. For the Romans at that time, this was the end of civiliza-*

Fan Theory Fun: Are all Stark Children Wargs?

48. Just a short drive from where Anthony got his Ph.D. and began his torrid but shameful love affair with Bimbi's fish 'n chips.

Night Gathers:
Warrior Monks, Wargs
and, like, a Wizard

tion; it was the end of the world. We know that there were Scots beyond the hills, but they didn't know that. . . . It could have been any kind of monster. It was the sense of this barrier against dark forces – it planted something in me. But when you write fantasy, every-thing is bigger and more colorful, so I took the Wall and made it three times as long and 700 feet high, and made it out of ice.[49]

It was in a very real sense "the end of civilization." Beyond that wall all rights of citizenship, all imperial power, all social contracts ceased to exist. At least this is what a Roman soldier might have thought in the second century.

49. Sarah Scott, "Game of Thrones Writer Reveals Hadrian's Wall Inspired Hit TV Series," thejournal. co.uk, 2014.

Hadrian's Wall: Hadrian's Wall east of Cawfields quarry, Northumberland. Hadrian's Wall, once completed, appeared smooth and whitewashed. From far away it looked like a newly spun, white ribbon along fields of green. It wasn't made of ice, but both Martin's Wall and Hadrian's Wall stood out as bright and striking. Photograph by Velella; courtesy of Wikimedia Commons.

There is almost no feature of Martin's landscape more important than the Wall. Besides its ability to keep the chief antagonists at bay (thereby establishing a key plot point), the Wall alienates two crucial cultures in *A Game of Thrones.* It is the relationship between the Night's Watch and the Free Folk that creates the necessary canvas for Jon Snow's development. Given that Martin devotes more point-of-view chapters to Jon than any other character, the significance of the Wall cannot be understated. In sum, the tension between crow and wildling allows Martin to explore Jon's duality.

No doubt, a similar tension existed between Romans and the "barbarians" beyond Hadrian's border. Even if the plot of *A Game of Thrones* hadn't been blue-printed, Martin had his finger on a key dynamic that would fuel his engine. The Wall is the primary example of Martin's literary process. It has been borrowed from a dramatic moment in history and super-charged with magic.

In our introduction to volume 1, we wrote that *religion is crucially important for the ice-and-fire tapestry.* Martin is in the business of creating religion *because he can't borrow from history without it.* This is obviously true with inventions like the Faith of the Seven and lupine spirit animals. But it is no less true with inventions like the Wall. Hadrian's Wall was built to forward a divine legacy.

In a sandstone artifact dated to ca. 118 CE, the following is said of Hadrian: The "necessity of keeping intact the empire [within its borders] had been imposed upon him by divine instruction."[50] In other words, Hadrian's motives (or so the political spin would have us believe) were given to him by the gods.

Bird's-Eye View: Hadrian's Wall

50. Anthony Everitt, *Hadrian and the Triumph of Rome* (New York: Random House, 2009), 222.

We would guess that Martin hadn't considered the theological significance of Hadrian's Wall on that day in 1981. This is exactly our point: borrowing anything of significance from premodern history is going to bring divine baggage along with it.

The Great Stallion
versus the Godswife

A PROTEST OF BROMOSAPIEN MASCULINITY

10

"The world in the past has been ruled by force, and man has dominated over woman by reason of his more forceful and aggressive qualities both of body and mind. But the balance is already shifting—force is losing its weight and mental alertness, intuition, and the spiritual qualities of love and service, in which woman is strong, are gaining ascendancy."

—ʿABDUʾL-BAHÁ

Distinctive Elements (Dothraki)
- henotheism
- fusion of spirituality and praxis
- hegemonic masculinity
- prominent pectorals

Distinctive Elements (Lhazareen)
- monotheism
- fusion of spirituality and praxis
- ritualized therapy
- perpetually bad hair days

Key Adherents (Dothraki)
- Daenerys Targaryen
- Drogo

Key Adherents (Lhazareen)
- Mirri Maz Duur
- Ornela (show only)

*The Great Stallion
versus the Godswife:
A Protest of Bromosapien
Masculinity*

W E'VE ALL BEEN there. You're pregnant, on horseback, and your husband decides to pit stop at Lhazar. Lhazar is just southeast of Vaes Dothrak and you're happy to be beyond the Dothraki Sea. But you're a bit conflicted because your husband's horde of murderous marauders is marauding and murdering. This might seem unruly to some, but the "bro" culture of the horde doesn't recognize the humanity of foreign villagers. You'd better be a pro-bro, rough-riding bareback at the brodeo if you want to be a bromosapien, *bro.*

Your back is killing you and your morning sickness is oppressive. Even so, you step in to stop the violent death of an elderly Lhazareen woman. You save her life, but your act of benevolence leads to a long sequence of catastrophes, landing you in the Red Waste without water, provisions, or protection.

Do you: (a) travel north, backtracking through Lhazar, (b) head west to slave-trading Yunkai, or (c) venture east to Bayasabhad, home of the deadliest women in Essos? The correct answer is (d) move south to Qarth. But once there, you may be forced to leave their greatest city in ruins and begin your quest for world domination. Pack accordingly.

DEEP DIVE: MIRRI AND BROSEPH

W E MEAN NO disrespect to Khal Drogo. He's our Khal, too. His fragrantly oiled man-braid is the inspiration for at least nineteen Kanye poems. The maesters calibrate their instruments using Drogo's perfectly circular nipples.

But (and we offer this criticism with all due respect) the androcentric culture of his horde is sometimes problematic.

If you want to know about the rituals, beliefs, and worship of the Dothraki, you'll have to talk to their neighbors. There are two reasons for this.

First, Martin introduces the horselords, their warriors, the Dosh Khaleen (council of widows), etc. all from the perspective of Daenerys. Dany is an outsider. Moreover, she is married to this culture against her will. As readers, our understanding of Dothraki culture grows as Dany's love for Khal Drogo grows. Khal Drogo initially presents as Attila the Hun who is truly—deep down—a Tickle-me Elmo in war paint. Who wouldn't be charmed by this gangster with a heart of gold? And once charmed, both Dany and the reader begin to accept Dothraki culture for its internal logic and normalcy within Martin's world. The Dany-Drogo love child is prophesied to be the khal who will unite all khals under his rule for the purpose of world domination. The baby in Dany's womb is called *the stallion who mounts the world*. Never mind that in Dothraki culture the word "mounts" is a euphemism for rape.[51] Somehow we want to overlook the mission of this fetal monster because, well, Drogo and Dany are just so damn cute together.[52]

Second, the stallion-worshipping ideals of Dothraki culture (what we're calling bromosapien masculinity) are only fully exposed by another outsider. Mirri Maz Duur is a Lhazareen priestess who offers a feminist critique of the Dothraki. She also turns out to be a demon-consorting, child-sacrificing bogeywoman. In short, she's a *maegi,* a practitioner of blood magic. By way of a typical Martin empathy-fork, we realize that our heroes are villainous and our villains possess virtue. In

Deep Dive:
Mirri and Broseph

51. In case your Dothraki is a bit rusty, we'll provide a refresher course below.

52. We're thinking of getting matching "moon of my life" and "my sun and stars" bathrobes.

the case of Mirri Maz Duur, we are forced to ask the basic question: *who, after all, is the real bad guy in this showdown between blood magic and bromosapien masculinity?*

The cultures of the Dothraki and the Lhazareen are as different as Klingons and *Flight of the Concords.* At least this is true at first glance. No doubt, the horselords and "Lamb Men" are meant to be contrasted. But—at the risk of offending both cultures—let's consider a few common characteristics.

The Great Stallion versus the Godswife: A Protest of Bromosapien Masculinity

Sleipnir: This stone in Gotland, Sweden (ca. 9th century) depicts Odin riding eight-legged Sleipnir. Horse deities feature in mythologies almost globally. Among Eurasian and Indo-European nomads, horse gods were a key focus of worship.

Both the Dothraki and Lhazareen are married to the land and to the natural lifecycles of their venerated beasts. In Vaes Dothrak, the culture is hinged on horse rearing, horse care, and the use of horses for everything from food production to warfare. It makes sense, then, that their mythology and rituals relate to the god of their people, the Great Stallion. Likewise, the bucolic life of the Lhazareen is tied closely to the worship of the Great Shepherd. In both cases, there is little (if any) distinction between sacred and secular. Sacred space, ritual, and mythology are integral to the life of these cultures.

Another similarity is the consecrated station of female elders. Temples dedicated to the Great Shepherd are mediated by "godswives" who function loosely as priestesses (*Game* 61, Daenerys VII). Although the analogy isn't perfect, the Dothraki employ the widows of dead khals within a council of female elders called the Dosh Khaleen. This council is the governing body of Vaes Dothrak. The Dosh Khaleen also appears to have some role in prophecy in Dothraki culture (S01E06, "A Golden Crown"). On the side of the Lhazareen, Mirri Maz Duur functions as more than a godswife; she might also speak prophetically (*Game* 61, Daenerys VIII).[53] These female leaders are not just glorified Luna Lovegoods. They function as powerbrokers of their respective societies and exert influence within Martin's plot.

But Martin's world is never simple; it's never as progressive as we'd like and too often it is unnervingly brutal. So, sweet summer child, don't be fooled by the power of the Dosh Khaleen. This group of crones may be made of powerful women but they reinforce a ritualized patriarchy.[54] For example, Daenerys must go before the Dosh Khaleen because she is pregnant with the child of a khal. To ensure the strength, bravery, and health of her fetus, she must participate in a ceremony governed by the women. The main event involves Dany eating the entire heart of a stallion. If she fails to eat the entire heart, her child might be "stillborn, deformed," or—and keep in mind this is a worst-case scenario—"female" (*Game* 61, Daenerys V).[55] We imagine *female* in this context is pronounced with decidedly Ferengi intonation.

Deep Dive:
Mirri and Broseph

53. The so-called "prophecy" of Mirri Maz Duur is a point of controversy among readers.

54. That's right: A.Ron and Anthony are insufferable cucks.

55. See also our discussion of ancient physiognomy in volume 1.

Scholars of gender studies will recognize this as the calling card of "hegemonic masculinity" (in this context, read: *bromosapien*). The ideal male in Dothraki culture is swift, strong, a fighter; other men will line up behind a man like this. Think Frank Sinatra, Frank Underwood, or really, any Frank.[56] Anything less than the bromosapien ideal embodies "subordinate masculinity." This includes, according to the wisdom of the Dothraki, a man who cannot sit a horse, a deformed man, or a weak man. From this point of view, being born female predetermines subordination. Being less than a horseman means being less than human.

Martin captures the misogynistic reality (of various ancient and modern cultures) that having a few women in power does not ensure the general well-being of all women. Indeed, the Dosh Khaleen reinforces the equine inequality.

In the bromosapien culture of the Dothraki, being a strong rider is paramount. The name of the group is derived from the word *dothrak*, which literally means "rider." But the gender specific language "man who rides" might be closer to the mark. To illustrate this point, consider this: the cognate verb *dothralat* can mean either "to ride alongside" or "to have an erection."[57] The language of the culture reinforces the assumption that the ideal Dothraki is a male who rides and rumbusticates (rumbusticate is an archaic English verb that means to hook up; it is a lovely word and deserves a second life). We also see this ideal reflected in the mythology of the group. Their divinity is decidedly male. It's not the Mighty Mare, bro; it's the title *Great Stallion (Vezhof).*[58]

Martin also captures the reality of a gendered landscape. In many cultures, certain spaces were designated for women. In the Ancient Near East, for example, these

56. Not Frank Stallone.

57. Richard Littauer, *The Dothraki Language Dictionary* (ver 3.11), Jan. 23, 2016; http://docs.dothraki.org/Dothraki.pdf. Relatedly, a synonym for rider is sajak. Cognate to this word is the verb *sajat*, meaning "to mount."

58. According to their mythology, the stars are horses of fire that gallop through the sky (*Game* 61, Daenerys v). After death, men who are properly burned on a funerary pyre can rise with the smoke to join the Great Stallion's riders (S02E02, "The Night Lands"). The afterlife is thought of as the "Night Lands."

were usually isolated domestic settings. Conversely, public spaces, the wilderness, interface with other tribes, etc. were all designated as male-specific landscapes. While we shouldn't take the comparison too far, the Dosh Khaleen is relatively insular while the male-dominated khalessars are free to range. As a case in point, once a khal dies, his wife *(khalisee)* must join the Dosh Khaleen and remain with them for the rest of her life. This is true whether or not she wants it. In Vaes Dothrak, women—even ruling-class women—are confined to a designated space. It is also common for sacred locations to be gendered. For example, the "Mother of Mountains" is considered holy by the Dothraki and only men are permitted there (*Game* 36, Daenerys IV).

Deep Dive:
Mirri and Broseph

Another way that landscape can be gendered is to speak of the land or soil as feminine. The natural counterpart here is that seeds are masculine. This is heard in the Dothraki word for seed (elain), which is the same word for semen (elain).[59] Such language reinforces the idea that women—like soil—are valuable insomuch as they are fertile. With this in mind, consider the Dothraki creation myth. They believe that a thousand years ago, the first man emerged riding the first horse from a lake named the "Womb of the World." This lake is rumored to be bottomless. While pregnant, Dany ritually washes in the great vagina lake but is able to tap the bottom (*Game* 61, Daenerys V). So the Dothraki have incorporated gendered landscapes into their mythology and rituals.

59. Littauer, *Language;* http://docs. dothraki.org/Dothraki.pdf.

If Dothraki riders are examples of bromosapien masculinity, their perspective on the Lhazareen gives us an even better example of what scholars of gender call "subordinate masculinity." The Lhazareen are derisively called "Lamb Men."[60] As subordinates, men are reduced to the categories of meekness, boyhood, or servitude.

60. "Lamb Men" is a sort of a lazy insult in our opinion. Why not *baaah*-barians?

These categories tend to be viewed as substandard. It's not uncommon for the language of subordination to include feminized insults. In modern parlance, the insults "little girl," "pussy," and "bitch" demonstrate the problem. The latter two examples also have the zoomorphic connotations of cats and female dogs.

Christ, the Good Shepherd: Mural of the Good Shepherd: In the Catacomb of Priscilla, Rome this mural might date as early as the third century. Notice that Jesus is beardless and without flowing robes (made iconic in later art). The shepherding theme is one of the earliest and most popular images for Jesus in visual art.

Something very much like this is happening in the insult "Lamb Men." Not only does this slur call out the primary way of life for the Lhazareen (they tend flocks), it also belittles their belief in a divine Shepherd. Indeed the Lhazareen believe that all people, of every tribe,

76

belong to the Great Shepherd who protects and punishes according to their deeds. The Dothraki, however, show no fear of the Lhazareen or their deity. From the bromosapien perspective, the Lamb Men are subordinate. Weakness is seen as cause enough for dehumanization.

Contrary to this worldview—indeed the contrast is striking—is the theology of Lhazareen monotheism. The godswives of Lhazar function primarily as priestesses and healers. Because the Great Shepherd is the god of all tribes, this deity cares for all. The Godswives are thus motivated to tend to the wounds of their enemies as well as their own.

This brings us to Mirri Maz Duur. She is a godswife who claims to be sent to heal all people, no matter where she might find them (*Game* 61, Daenerys VII). Her theology is that all tribes share a common humanity and are deserving of care.

Deep Dive:
Mirri and Broseph

Excursus: Prophets and Tricksters

Sacred traditions always ebb and flow between pure observance and prophetic movement. Most of the time, this ebb and flow is a necessary process of order and disorder, with the hope for a new and improved order. Prophetic voices— from Jeremiah to Martin Luther King—challenge traditional power structures and belief systems. Every now and then, however, a prophet comes along who wants to burn the entire system to the ground. Along these lines, we meet the mythological "trickster."[61]

The trickster's job is to test the resilience of sacred structures. Whether it is Loki of Norse

61. Trickster is a technical term in comparative mythology. He (usually it's a "he") can vacillate between kindness and cruelty, help and hindrance, immaturity and wisdom. In several cultures—notable in African and Native American mythology—the trickster is also a shapeshifter.

*The Great Stallion
versus the Godswife:
A Protest of Bromosapien
Masculinity*

fame or Coyote of Navajo tradition, the trickster will utterly ruin your sandcastle if left unchecked. Worse, (s)he will laugh in your face while doing it. Mirri Maz Durr doesn't meet all of the typical criteria for a trickster (e.g., she isn't a shapeshifter) but she does meet a few: (1) she deceives with a trick; (2) she turns a plot on its head; (3) she speaks for a god; (4) she laughs cruelly at Dany when she reveals her magic trick (*Game* 68, Daenerys IX). It might also be worth noting that Pan (a satyr) is known for his trickster qualities. In Greek mythology, Pan is also the god of shepherds and flocks.

Mirri probably fits more comfortably within the prophet category but she's got a few tricks up her sleeve too. One of the great fan debates is the interpretation of her words to Dany about when Drogo will return "as he was." Was she speaking prophetically (i.e. foretelling the future, J. K. Rowling-style) or was she simply telling Dany "never" in poetic language? Fans will have to wait to see whether Mirri is prophetess or trickster. Our guess is that she is a combination of both. After all, prophets don't always foretell the future; sometimes they simply speak truth to power.

If indeed Mirri Maz Duur is a trickster, Martin executes the plot flip brilliantly. Mirri is introduced as an altruistic representative of a peaceful people. After being saved and adopted by Dany, the godswife volunteers to treat Khal Drogo's wound. At first glance, the healer steps in just in time to solve Dany's most immediate problem. Dany is undoubtedly in love with Drogo at this point in the story. Her precious "Sun and Stars" is seriously

78

injured. In order for the love story to continue, Dany's love interest must survive. Fortunately Dany has saved the life of a godswife whose primary purpose in life is to heal *(a typical plot progression)*. It doesn't occur to Dany that this godswife might be acting as an agent of divine disorder *(the plot flip)*.

Deep Dive: Mirri and Broseph

We now arrive at the one of the darkest and most complicated problems with Martin's worldbuilding. The fact of the matter is that the culture of the Dothraki is a culture of institutionalized rape, murder, and slavery. The horselords regularly range to neighboring tribes to steal their resources (including people who are sold into slavery). If the horde is able to subdue the village, the riders rape the village women—they call it "mounting"—as a reward for their efforts. As we witness the aftermath of a ravaged village through Dany's eyes, she internalizes the conflict. She witnesses ritualized post-battle rape and attempts to steel herself against her repulsion.

Dany tells herself that this is part of war. As she aims to bring war (eventually) to Westeros, she tells herself to accept it. Her internal dialogue suggests that she means to conquer and she will continue to pursue the Iron Throne even if the rituals of war repulse her. Eventually Dany decides to intercede and save at least a few Lazareen women from assault. To "save" them, she claims these women as her own slaves to end the violence (*Game* 61, Daenerys VII).

Martin's fans love the complexity of his world. Going a step further, most will grant that war is morally complex. But is rape? Is slavery? And if we decide to pound our fists and reject these wartime realities as evil, how do we justify our empathy with Daenerys? Isn't Dany's lust for power a progenitor of violence? Isn't her belief that she has ruling-class blood in her veins just as insidious as any ethical problem we might encounter in this story?

This is when Mirri Maz Duur approaches center stage. If we, the readers, have failed to pound our fists at the notion of *a stallion who mounts the world,* the ravaged godswife will do it for us.

HISTORICAL BACKDROP: ATTILA THE HUN

FROM A ROMAN perspective, the mid 5th century was all about Attila the Hun. Attila went from relative obscurity to the most feared man in the world, leading the Roman historian Jordanes to write: "He was a man born into the world to shake the nations, the scourge of all lands, who in some way terrified all mankind by the dreadful rumors noised abroad concerning him."[62] Attila believed himself to be the "scourge of God."

62. William Stearns Davis, ed., *Readings in Ancient History: Illustrative Extracts from the Sources,* 2 Vols. (Boston: Allyn and Bacon, 1912-1913), 322.

The Huns approaching Rome: Artist Ulpiano Checa (1897) depicts Attila invading Italy. Courtesy of Wikimedia Commons.

After bringing the great empire of Rome to its knees (except Constantinople), Attila accepted peace for a hefty cost. Rome paid annually and the cost went up steadily year by year. In 440 CE alone, the Roman tribute was 700 pounds of solid gold. Attila was a savvy ruler and a fierce warrior on the battlefield. He murdered his own brother (who had ruled jointly with him for a time) but treated his son tenderly. And, as rumors have it, his wives were innumerable.

There are a few notable parallels between the Huns of this era and the Dothraki. The Huns emerged from a nomadic people known for their prowess as horseback warriors. This, of course, sounds a lot like the ranging hordes of the Dothraki. The tribute paid to the Dothraki by Pentos is similar to that levied against Rome. In other words, these western societies were paying to not be raided. We also see at least one obvious connection between Drogo and Attila. One rumor about Attila's death is intriguing: he was murdered in his marriage bed by his young bride (historically speaking, this rumor is probably false). Drogo meets his final demise at the hands of his own young bride. While it was a mercy killing, Dany does indeed smother Drogo to death in his bed.

It is also interesting that Attila once demanded half of Western Europe as a dowry to betroth himself to Honoria (sister of Emperor Valentinian III).[63] Ultimately Honoria agreed to marry someone else but Attila invaded Italy anyway. While this parallel is on the weak side, Khal Drogo promised to invade Westeros to demonstrate his love and devotion for Dany. In Drogo's case, he did indeed marry his betrothed but did not survive long enough to keep his promise.

63. Honoria—like Dany—was matched to a wealthy man but did not want to marry him. So she sent word to Attila (whom Valentinian III feared) for a solution to her betrothal. Attila responded by claiming that he would marry Honoria instead. Honoria—unlike Dany—then had a choice between two husbands. She claimed that Attila had misunderstood her request and agreed to marry the original man chosen for her by her brother.

Given these parallels, we might also consider the prophecy that Drogo's son will "mount the world." Do we hear an echo of Attila, the man "born into the world to shake the nations"?

CHARACTER STUDIES: KHAL JOMMO AND ORNELA

THE CONSEQUENCES OF Dothraki gender expectations can be seen in the contrast of two minor characters. One is a book character, a Dothraki khal; the other is a show-only character, a young Lhazareen widow. In *Game* we meet Khal Jommo, who is among the more powerful khals of the Dothraki. He has four wives. If we use gendered landscape language to understand his worldview, we could use the analogy of a man with four fields, resulting in four times the produce. In a world where raiders are highly valued, more sons means more resources. Khals are free—indeed expected—to range beyond borders and take resources from other tribes. This may include the taking of people to be sold/traded into slavery. The fact that he has four wives illustrates the almost borderless freedom of Dothraki men. Both villages and people are seen as property to be taken. Because the Dothraki choose to take from others to grow their resources (they are not farmers) the importance of their male progeny and slave trading is central. They show great affinity to the Ironborn, who infamously "do not sow." And if they ever learn of the Ironborn's slogan, they'll probably steal that too.

Contrast this with Ornela, a young member of the Dosh Khaleen that Daenerys meets in Vaes Dothrak. Ornela—who is Lhazareen—is married to a khal at the age of twelve. When she fails to produce a boy (i.e. she gave birth to a girl), her husband breaks her ribs. She is widowed at sixteen and forced to live out her life with the Dosh Khaleen. When she meets Dany, Ornela begins to express her discontent with her lot in life but seems resolved to remain enslaved until she is offered a way out (S06E04, "The Book of the Stranger"). Ornela's marriage is little more than an act of institutionally sanctioned human trafficking. That she is abused for giving birth to the wrong gender reinforces the very limited value she has within the Dothraki culture. She is seen as a resource that has failed to produce. Finally, she isn't simply enslaved by a single man. Her bondage exists within a ritualized social structure. Even though her life within the Dosh Khaleen is relatively comfortable, she remains a slave.

Character Studies: Khal Jommo and Ornela

CHARACTER STUDY: DAARIO NAHARIS

THE FIRST AND most important thing to know about Daario Naharis is that he's quite fetching. If his come-hither-bedroom-baby blues aren't enough to make you tingle, behold the gleaming gold tooth in that seductive smile. Indeed, he might just flash you a devil-may-care smolder after he rolls a severed head your way. Not into precious metal in the grill, you say? Can we interest you in his dyed-blue trident beard? Or his equally smurfy Jheri curl? *Okay, fine. . .* Daario is an acquired taste. But Dany thinks he's a burning beacon of raw sexuality. And that, as far as we can tell, is 90% of the Meereenese plot for *A Dance of Dragons.*[64]

The gist of it is that Dany decides to rule Meereen while distracted by a sexpot sellsword who becomes her

64. Don't let Martin fool you; it's really not that complicated.

boyfriend. There are assassinations, lost dragons, political debates about slavery and fighting pits. But none of these problems occupy her thoughts more than Daario. Even when he's away, she visualizes him and his strong hands. She imagines him fondling the hilts of his weapons (golden hilts shaped like naked women) and realizes that she is jealous of his arakh and stiletto (*Dance* 11, Daenerys 11). After all, she is still a teenager. Dany may be wise beyond her years, but what young adult isn't motivated by biology? If Dany has a "type" at this point in the story, it's a cross between Wild Bill Hickok and Ravishing Rick Rude.[65]

For readers frustrated with Dany's long delay in Meereen, Daario is just a roadblock in the way of the plot. We admit that our kneejerk opinions of the Dany-Daario tryst were pretty low. But there might be another way to think about Daario that gives Martin a bit more credit for character development. Of course, we're not talking about Daario's development (he's a mere Meereenese mimbo) but he's important for what he does for Dany's character arc.

During her sojourn with the Dothraki, Dany embraces her role as Drogo's khaleesi and must participate in all of the religious rites of passage required of her. She even burns Drogo on a funeral pyre when the time comes.[66] After Drogo is gone, she asks Aggo, Jhogo, and Rakharo to be her bloodriders. She has clearly internalized (and adapted) a number of Dothraki traditions. But eventually—if she means to rule—she needs to become more than a khaleesi. In a religion where a woman is worth less than a good horse, the ceiling for a khaleesi is pretty low (even one who is fire made flesh). In a sense, Dany uses Daario to lose her religion. And she

65. Yes, this was a real guy. Do a youtube search.

66. Admittedly, funerary pyres are features of both Targaryen and Dothraki tradition.

84

doesn't just lose her religion. In our opinion, she turns it upside down.

By Dothraki standards, Daario is the ideal man. He is a talented warrior. No less than Barristan Selmy regards Daario as courageous and talented in battle (*Winds,* Barristan 1). Daario is a fighter and a lover. Most notably, he's an accomplished horseman.[67] He boasts that he can sleep in his saddle while afield (*Dance* 43, Daenerys VII). He also boasts that he can outride an arrow (*Dance* 36, Daenerys VI). *Cue eye roll.* Now consider the fact that "Nahar" is the name of Tolkien's mythological horse deity. If ever there was a non-Dothraki man designed to represent the Dothraki ideal, it's Daario Naharis.

He is, therefore, the perfect guy for Dany to reverse gender rolls with. There is no doubt that she's smitten with him. But she demonstrates almost complete power in this relationship. In sum, she chooses Daario, uses him as she pleases, and then discards him when she's ready to move on. At the end of *Dance*, she has forced him into the service of the Yunkai'i (he becomes a hostage in a deal that brings peace). This is a full turn for Dany who was once herself traded in a deal between Viserys and Drogo. Whereas she was once traded like a horse, she now becomes the horse trader.

Character Study:
Daario Naharis

67. In the HBO adaptation, Daario's character is merged with Belwas (the barrel-bellied fighting former slave). This is something of an awkward merger because Belwas is notably dismissive of "horseboys" who "jingle when they die" (*Clash* 63, Daenerys V). Belwas bests the horsed Meereen champion in single combat without taking a mount or armor. In the HBO series, this feat is accomplished by Daario, who claims that horses are stupid (S04E03, "Breaker of Chains"). This is something Belwas might say in the books, not Daario.

FAN THEORY FUN: LET'S ALL OVERANALYZE DANY'S WOMB

Daenerys Targaryen is a prophecy bull's-eye. Whether the topic is her child, her khal, or herself, people toss prophetic utterances at her like she's the last player on a spooky dodgeball team. As the subject of much prophecy, she is also fan theory magnet. It's not easy being a leading candidate for prince(ss) that was promised.

In one of Dany's most important transitional chapters, she demands to know when Drogo will be as he was. Mirri responds with three symbolic portents. Drogo will be as he was when:

(a) the sun rises in the west and sets in the east

(b) the seas go dry and

(c) mountains blow in the wind like leaves

(d) Dany's womb quickens again and she bears a living child

Mirri concludes, "Then he will return, and not before" (*Game* 46, Daenerys IX). At first glance, this seems to be nothing more than a sick burn at Dany's expense, a flowery way to say, "uhhh… how about *never*, huh? How about *that?!*" It reads as a litany of things that can never conceivably happen. And it was seen as such for years within the fandom.

But by the end of *Dance* the fan hive mind noticed that some of these conditions had been met, if one is willing to do a bit of mental gymnastics.

(a) DoranMartell sent his son Quentin from west to east to form a marriage alliance with Dany, where he was roasted alive by dragon fire. The sigil for the Martell is a sun punctured by a spear (hence the name, Sunspear). So, in Martin's world, at least one "sun" traveled from west to east.

(b) Daenerys observes in Dance that the grassy plains the Dolthraki call their "sea" is starting to dry and die off, apparently in advance of the change in season.

(c) The fate of the "mountains" might refer to Gregor Clegane's nickname and his defeat, agonizing death, and ensuing un-life. Or they could refer to the

smoking remains of the Meereen pyramids, which Vise-
rion and Rhaegal have turned into their roosts.

If you find these supposed "fulfillments" compelling, you'll be looking for a comeback performance from
Dany's womb.[68] All that remains is for Dany to deliver
a living child. At the end of *Dance* she appears to suffer
a miscarriage, so the prophecy remains unfulfilled. But
what if Daenerys has a child and names him/her Drogo
to honor her ex-husband? In your *face*, Mirri. *The stallion
who mounts the world* is back on the table.

Now, you might ask: will any of this actually bring
back Khal Drogo "as he was"? We won't begrudge you
a bit of healthy doubt. But let's not ruin the fun of those
who are heavily invested in the return (in some form)
of Drogo. Before moving on, we will leave you with one
simple question: *knowing what we know of Dany's character development, do you think she even wants Drogo back?*

FAN THEORY FUN (PART 2):
FETUS FIXATION

HOLD ON TO your tinfoil hats as we introduce
the awesomestrosity of all fan theories![69] This
is the Tyrion-as-time-traveling-fetus theory
and it comes with a health warning. Some who have
adopted this theory have spiraled into insanity or gone
into a fake fugue state *à la* Walter White. Side effects
include dry mouth, greyscale, and/or a circa 2004 blog
that only relatives read. Also, do not read this fan theory
while pregnant.

In its most basic form, this is the idea: Tyrion is the
son of Daenerys, making him a secret Targaryen and a
dragon-riding time bandit . . . no, seriously, hear us out.
Mirri Maz Duur's blood magic split the fabric of space

*Character Study:
Daario Naharis*

68. Interestingly, the topic of
Dany's womb is a featured topic
in season 7 . . . *not that it's any of
Tyrion's damned business!*

69. We've done a bit of our own
chemistry here, but the pioneer of
this theory is redditor "xyseth" in a
thread titled "D+D=T - a never-be-
fore-seen theory," Mar. 28, 2015.

and time. The magic sent Dany's actual fetus back into Joanna Lannister's womb, becoming Tyrion. Meanwhile, the long dead fetus of Joanna and Tywin's actual son in the former timeline was brought back to the future.[70] Tyrion lives for approximately 30 years as a Lannister, kills his surrogate father, crosses the Narrow Sea, and returns to Dany to help her conquer the world.

We begin with the circumstances of Mirri's blood-magic ritual, which ends with Dany losing her child and Drogo losing his personality (and eventually his life). When Mirri delivers Dany's child, it is described as "monstrous… twisted… scaled like a lizard, blind, with the stub of a tail and small leather wings like the wings of a bat." The child appears to have been dead and in the grave for years, "inside he was full of grave worms and the stink of corruption" (*Game* 68, Daenerys IX).

This is gruesome, to be sure, but not unprecedented in the Targaryen family tree. Rhaenyra Targaryen also suffered a stillborn child, who was similarly described as having dragonish features.[71] The lines that most inspire this theory are about the baby being dead for years, and the similarity to Tyrion's appearance at birth.

Baby Tyrion is rumored to be monstrous, with a tail, an evil eye, lion's claws, sharp teeth, and possessing both male and female genitalia. Prince Oberyn confirms hearing the rumors but is disappointed to find Tyrion to be a normal baby (S04E07, "Mockingbird"). While it's easy to believe this is just cruel gossip, perhaps there is more to it.

Let's grant that Daenarys's fetus did look something like baby Tyrion. We know that Martin's world plays with the idea of time travel from time to time. Indeed, we know a particular greenseer named Bran Stark who can project himself into the past. Now consider this: just before Dany gives birth, she sees dancing shapes

---

The Great Stallion versus the Godswife: A Protest of Bromosapien Masculinity

70. Apologies to Robert Zemeckis. You didn't deserve to be dragged into this.

71. Rhaenyra's child was "a stillborn girl, twisted and malformed, with a hole in her chest where her heart should have been, and a stubby, scaled tail" (*Fire and Blood*, "The Dying of the Dragons").

inside the tent. "She glimpsed the shadow of a great wolf, and another like a man wreathed in flames" (*Game* 64, Daenerys VIII). Yeah, yeah, we know. It's probably not Bran Stark and Jon Snow who have come from the future to save Tyrion and bring him into the past. That would be absurd.

It might be even more to absurd to suggest that Tyrion's saddle-making prowess is a call back to the Dothraki ideal that a great warrior must be able to sit a horse. And it would be sheer nonsense to suggest that Martin is building up to an event whereby Tyrion invents a saddle that allows him to ride a dragon into battle (thus fulfilling the stallion-who-mounts-the-world prophecy). Yes, such foolishness would break all the rules of logic. But it would certainly adhere to the rule of cool.

If you're still reading this, you may be interested in a few literary hints that Tyrion has dragon blood flowing through his veins. Tyrion grew up having dreams of being a Targaryen prince and riding dragons, soaring through the skies. For his birthday, he once asked for a little dragon, not knowing they had died out (S06E02, "Home"; show only). Dreams of dragons and the future are common among Targaryens. Tyrion knows an immense amount of dragon lore, as revealed when Griff commands him to begin writing a history of dragons (*Dance* 14, Tyrion IV). Tyrion's physical appearance is also Targaryen-ish. His blonde hair is described as more platinum than the gold Lannisters are famous for. He also has mismatched eye colors, a trait he shares with Shiera Seastar, a Targaryen bastard.[72]

The grosser variants of this theory add a bit of Oedipus complex into the mix. Some fans have suggested that Tyrion will wed Dany and become the *stallion who mounts his mom, and then, presumably, the world.* We

Fan Theory Fun (Part 2): Fetus Fixation

72. As far as the bastard part, one popular theory is that Tyrion is the child of the "mad king" Aerys and Joanna Lannister, the wife of Tywin. There are rumors throughout *Song* that Aerys had an infatuation with Joanna and used his power to take inappropriate liberties with Tywin's wife. She was also present at a tournament in King's Landing where Aerys made a vulgar remark about her breasts (*World*, "Aerys II"). Less than a year later, Joanna died in childbirth.

wouldn't put it past Martin. And Tyrion does in fact have a few similarities to Oedipus.[73]

The problems with this theory are legion. To begin with, just look at it. This theory is more monstrous than any dead fetus, and about as likely to pass a smell test. But before you judge too harshly, the fans haven't had a new book in a very long time, and the seventh season of *Game of Thrones* has sadly shut the door on the glorious idea of our three favorite heroes mounting our three favorite dragons and ushering in *A Dream of Spring*. At this point, we'd settle for the unending howl of *The Winds of Winter*.

BIRD'S-EYE VIEW: ÉOWYN AND MIRRI AS FIRST AND THIRD-WAVE FEMINISTS

THERE ARE ALL kinds of feminist critiques of traditional narratives and all kinds of ways to do it. Feminist criticism is, therefore, a lot like the game Twister (seriously, look it up). Let's just look at a single branch of the field: *feminist hermeneutics*. (A "hermeneutic" is a strategy for interpretation.) Feminist hermeneutics developed in conversation with religious studies as a way to challenge patriarchy. Sacred texts, from this perspective, are built on patriarchal biases (more often than not). So, of course, the default position of most traditional readers is going to be patriarchy.

But readers of sacred texts can choose to interpret them in new ways, ways that support the well-being of women. One possible feminist approach reads the voices of ancient men in conversation with the lived experiences of women. The relationship between ancient and modern voices often means a big middle finger to tradi-

The Great Stallion versus the Godswife: A Protest of Bromosapien Masculinity

73. (1) Both Tyrion and Oedipus save cities and then become hated by the people of those same cities;
(2) both are disowned by their fathers;
(3) both fathers consider infanticide;
(4) both end up killing their fathers. And here is the kicker:
(5) Tyrion, famously, has an abnormal gait; Oedipus literally means "swollen foot."

tion. Feminist readers, therefore, have the freedom to be "uncooperative readers." The hope is to use a method of reading (a feminist hermeneutic) to reinterpret sacred words and construct better worlds of meaning.

We trust that you'll keep this in mind as we put two of our favorite authors under the microscope: J. R. R. Tolkien and George R. R. Martin. Tolkien's work is something very much like a sacred text to fantasy readers. Tolkien's work—because it is so beloved and influential—is always going to invite vivisection. It is possible, therefore, to score cheap points by judging the author against contemporary feminist standards. That said, let's do a bit of now-versus-then comparison. Because in order to talk about Martin's female characters—especially among the Dothraki—we need to reflect a bit on the O.G. R. R.

Tolkien's plots generally depict bromance quests across Middle-earth. The author either neglects to include women's voices (e.g. *The Hobbit*) or he characterizes women as far too lofty to be empathetic (e.g. *Fellowship*). These two criticisms highlight widespread problems in androcentric literature: (1) either the woman doesn't exist in any meaningful way; or (2) the woman exists to support/complicate the development of a male character. We ought to keep in mind that Tolkien published *The Hobbit* in 1937 and *Fellowship* in 1954. It is also worth noting that Tolkien was environmentally conscious, progressive in terms of capital punishment, and a friend to Judaism when such a stance was unpopular. But even progressive men are still men made by the times they inhabit. Whatever other virtues he had, Tolkien was lacking in his humanization of women.

This backdrop makes Éowyn stand out as remarkable. Readers will remember Éowyn as the niece and

Bird's-Eye View: Éowyn and Mirri as First and Third-Wave Feminists

goddaughter of King Théoden. She is left in charge of Rohan in *The Return of the King,* essentially making her the queen regent of the horselords (Éowyn means "horse joy" in Old English). But because of the gender expectations of the Rohirrim, Éowyn is forbidden to ride to war. In a plot point akin to the historical Mulan (of the Han Dynasty), Éowyn disguises herself as a male and rides with the cavalry. During the battle at Pelennor Fields she stands between the wounded Théoden and the Witch-king of Angmar. The Witch-king quips, "Hinder me? Thou fool. No living man may hinder me!" Then Éowyn lands the great one-liner, "But no living man am I! You look upon a woman. Éowyn I am, Éomund's daughter. . . ." (*Return,* Book Five, VI). Then, with the help of her sidecar-hobbit friend, she slays one of baddest badasses of all of Arda. We could also look at characters like Galadriel and Lúthien (*Silmaril*) to find other exceptions to the rule.

The example of Éowyn is indeed exceptional. Tolkien's gender-bending plot twist still works for most readers even decades later. It's also a nod to first- and second-wave feminist ideals. Simply put, this is the 20th-century mantra, that women can do everything men can do, and often do it better. That Tolkien included this plot twist in a sea of Middle-earth brotagonists isn't nothing. Even so, third- and fourth-wave feminists will be less impressed with Tolkien's nod to progress. More recent voices of the movement are less inclined to remind us that Ginger Rogers danced backwards and in high heels.[74] Newer waves of feminism offer systematic criticism of bromosapien institutions.

74. Bob Thaves: "Sure he was great, but don't forget that Ginger Rogers did everything he did, ...backwards and in high heels." 1982 cartoon: reelclassics.com/Actresses/Ginger/ginger-article2.htm

Bird's-Eye View: Éowyn
and Mirri as First and
Third-Wave Feminists

Hua Mulan: This 18th century ink on silk painting depicts Hua Mulan in traditional garb. She is most famous for her legendary exploits as a warrior. Courtesy of Wikimedia Commons.

When Martin wrote in the 1990s, the feminist mantra was much less a proclamation that "women are strong" and much more a call to "turn the outrage into political power."[75] So while it is interesting that Martin's

75. Rebecca Walker, "Becoming the Third Wave," *Ms. Magazine,* 1992.

feministic critique of the Dothraki shows close parallels of Tolkien's bromosapien masculinity (and a 1950's subversion of it), we should anticipate a far different result from these plot twists. Éowyn proves herself brave and strong within the man-made social structure. This is enough to surprise Tolkien's target audience. Mirri Maz Duur is something else entirely. The godswife doesn't just prove her strength within the social structure, Mirri Maz Duur is ready and willing to burn the entire Stallion-worshipping hierarchy to the ground.

Finally, just as Tolkien was a man of his own era, Martin too is a man of his. No doubt many of his notions of masculinity are shaped by his social conditioning. If Martin's portraits of Daenerys, Mirri Maz Duur, and the Dosh Khaleen look like they are crafted by a 1990's male trying to think progressively, it is probably because that is who he was when *A Game of Thrones* took shape. This doesn't let him off the hook for his pornographic fascination with violence or his oversexed ideations. Younger generations of readers will continue to measure *A Song of Ice and Fire* against their own experiences of gender, power dynamics, and religion. This is the fate of every work that continues to be read. *It is known.*

Maritime Monstrosity

IRONBORN AND OTHER BLASPHEMOUS
FISH-FROGS OF NAMELESS DESIGN

11

Alive without breath,
As cold as death;
Never thirsty, ever drinking,
All in mail never clinking.

—GOLLUM

Distinctive Elements

- water immersion
- paying the iron price
- reaping what one certainly Did Not Sow
- Lovecraftian mythos

Key Adherents

- Theon Greyjoy
- Asha/Yara Greyjoy
- Aeron "Damphair" Greyjoy
- Euron Greyjoy
- all the damned Greyjoys, basically

TRAVEL GUIDE

SOMETIMES YOU JUST feel the call of freedom that can only be found on the open seas. When the cold embrace of the ocean beckons, there's only one cure: a cruise of the Iron Islands! Explore this stormy corner of the world in luxury and leave the piracy prevention to your captain and crew.

Nestled within Ironman's Bay just east of the romantic Sunset Sea, this rugged archipelago is waiting for you. Feast your eyes on the austere beauty of rugged black mountain ranges set against slate-gray skies. As the name Sunset Sea implies, each island offers breathtaking and unobstructed views of the sun going down over the horizon.

Looking for impressive architecture? Take a day trip to the ancestral castle of the Greyjoys. The fortress at Pyke commands the island of the same name. Still proud and mighty, the castle has been renovated and subdivided by nature as the waters have eroded its foundations. Some towers have been left broken and tottering but access to them can be had via loosely connected, swaying rope bridges. Bring the kids! These ruins are impressive, not in size or opulence, but for their stubborn refusal to collapse.

For the cryptozoologists out there, there's a lot of history and science to get to pseudoing! Explore ancient Old Wyk, which boasts the bones of Nagga, the greatest of all sea dragons. Locals believe that these bones are the petrified remains of the monster defeated by the Grey King, patriarch of the Ironborn. Or perhaps they are the pillars of a long abandoned fortress. *Who's to say?*

While exploring the outer islands, keep an eye out for the world-famous kraken! So much more than mythological, this gigantic cephalopod is capable of dragging the mightiest longship right down to Davey Jones' locker. Seriously, keep an eye out for those things. And if spotted, grab your trustiest harpoon, say a quick prayer to the Drowned God, and remember, what is dead may never die!

Pl. XXVI.   *T. 2. P. 256.*

Denys-Montfort del.   *E. Voysard S.*

LE POULPE COLOSSAL.

The Giant Octopus: Large sea monsters like this gigantic
octopus have been the subject of sailing legends for as long
as there have been sailors. This 1901 illustration by Pierre
Dénys de Montfort was inspired by French sailors who
claimed to have been attacked by it off the coast of Angola.
Courtesy of Wikimedia Commons.

*Maritime Monstrosity:
Ironborn and other
Blasphemous Fish-frogs
of Nameless Design*

76. Asha Greyjoy is the name of Theon's sister in the original story. She was renamed "Yara" in the HBO-adaptation. Theon's best hope is that Asha/Yara wins the Driftwood Crown. Not only does she maintain her affection for her brother, she has shaped up to be the "best" Greyjoy. She is a consummate Iron Islander in seamanship, leadership, and appetite. She also envisions a new era for the Ironborn of increased trade and political networking. She's a somewhat tragic Stringer Bell-type, seeing the inevitable end of the line for the "Old Way" and wanting to go legit before it's too late.

77. More on this deeply mysterious character below (you might be surprised by the result).

THEON IS THE rare character in Martin's world who is truly lost with no way home. Brought up as hostage at Winterfell, he will never be Ironborn in his father's eyes. After his treachery against the Starks, he will never be welcome in the North again. His plight worsens at the Dreadfort where he suffers to the point of complete identity erasure. Theon's only tether to the land of his birth is his sister Asha/Yara, who has herself been displaced.[76] Indeed Theon's only rival in rootlessness is Varys. Yet even Varys has learned to swim with the sharks of King's Landing.[77] Theon is simply adrift, barely surviving as the plaything of Ramsay Snow, that sadistic nihilist.

We would never wish for a child to be raised on the Iron Islands. Simply put, the chances of surviving such an upbringing are dismal. If you aren't lost at sea or in a raid, your baptism into the Ironborn religion involves being held below the waves until your lifeless body stops breathing. If you're lucky enough to cough up saltwater and survive, your reward is more hunger-motivated violence. And don't get us started on the Ironborn healthcare system. If you're sick or wounded, Ironborn physicians know only two treatments: fire or seawater. If these won't cure you, then (good news!) the Drowned God needs a new oarsman, and you just got drafted. Having said all that, Theon is one of the very few people in Westeros who would have had a better life had he remained at Pyke.

Theon doesn't seem to have any guardian angels looking out for him. Indeed, Greyjoys don't believe in such things. The closest things to angels in Ironborn theology are the mermaids that serve the drowned in the next life (*Feast* 1, "The Prophet"). Moreover, from an Ironborn perspective, Theon has spent too much of his life on the greenlands to be helped by the Drowned God.[78] He is, however, within reach of the Storm God, "a malignant deity who dwells in the sky and hates men and all their works" (*World*, "Iron Islands").[79]

78. The geographical difference between the islands and the rest of the North likely accounts for the difference in religion. Because the soil on the Iron Islands was very poor quality, weirwood never took hold there and the Children of the Forest never lived there. In this cultural vacuum, a different belief system emerged. The Ironborn were aware of something like a tree spirit, which they named "Ygg." A ygg was thought to be a carnivorous pale-wooded demon tree—perhaps an alternative mythology of the "old gods" (*World*, "Iron Islands").

79. Other than that, he's not so bad. You just don't know him like we do.

Neptune: Neptune is the Roman iteration of the Poseidon, the Greek god of waters. Both were divine governors of fresh water and oceans. This oil on canvas was painted by Andrea Doria ca. 1540-50. Courtesy of Wikamedia Commons.

The Storm God is the counterpart to the Drowned God. The two deities have been locked in mortal combat for a thousand thousand years. In Ironborn religion, the Storm God is responsible for the worst nightmares of sailors: storms that render the waves cold, black, and deadly. Very little is beyond the reach of his divine malice. Just imagine how he might accurse and afflict a renegade like Theon who is so far from the Sea.

The Drowned God, on the other hand, is Aegir, Neptune, and Ulmo all rolled into a single Creator deity. According to Iron Islands mythology, the Drowned God created the Ironborn in his own image. Iron Islanders, therefore, are superior beings with the license to take from the lesser mortals around them. Extending from their divine mandate the Ironborn believe they have been "blessed with steel." This is their religious justification for ravaging farms and villages. Rather than pay in gold, they "pay the iron price," which means murder and theft.[80]

80. Don't hate the player; hate the game, son.

Of course, this theology makes little sense to the other cultures of Westeros. Archmaester Haereg suggests that (like all other early humans in Westeros) the first Ironborn were simply First Men. When they colonized the islands, they probably discovered some nautical themed fragments from an earlier culture and adopted them as their own. Later, after discovering their islands were rich in iron (but poor in everything else), they turned to pragmatic piracy rather than agriculture. This, according to an alternative view, is how their tradition of raiding emerged. This way of life is now called the "Old Way." But if Haereg's theory holds water, it is a relatively new way painted with mythology to support their absurdly antisocial policies (*World*, "The Iron Islands").

When Theon finally returns to Pyke after years away, he's forgotten the Old Way. King Balon asks his son how he paid for the gold around his neck. Sheepishly, Theon admits that he bought it rather than paying "with iron" (*Clash* 11, Theon 1; S02E02, "The Night Lands"). As a boy raised by Ned Stark—a famously honorable man— Theon doesn't take jewelry from men he's murdered. Theon has been socialized with Stark sensibilities and is therefore an alien to Greyjoy culture. The best he can do is try to become half the man his sister is. Upon realizing this, Theon becomes desperate and decides to sack Winterfell to prove himself.

Deep Dive: Nautical Nihilism

From the Stark perspective, Theon's sacking of Winterfell is unforgivable. But from the Greyjoy perspective, if you need a thing, you pay the iron price for it. Theon chooses to take what he needs with iron and steel. He tries to buy his father's love and a way home. Tragically, the currency of Pyke isn't accepted at Winterfell.

Excursus: Drowned Men

The religion of the Drowned God is stubbornly resistant to being absorbed or co-opted by other foreign religions. Andal invaders repeatedly failed to contaminate the Ironborn with the doctrine of the Seven. The first sept built on the Iron Islands was quickly destroyed by a violent faction of Drowned Men (priests of the Drowned God). These priests discouraged worship by using swords to hack up would-be converts (*World*, "The Iron Islands"). It was also extremely difficult to sell them "coexist" bumper stickers as there was no market for them and the Ironborn preferred to pay the "iron price" anyway (thus discouraging salesmen of all sorts).

81. Don't try this at home.

82. In one legend, the priests crowned a fellow Drowned Man named Lodos. He was a barefooted holy man who styled himself as the son of the Drowned God. Once while mounting a defense against invaders, Lodos called on krakens of the deep to pull down his enemies' ships. When this failed, he packed stones into his robes and sunk himself into the ocean to discuss the matter with his father, the Drowned God (*Fire and Blood*, "The Reign of the Dragon"). That was the end of his reign. Lesson learned: generally speaking, is it a bad idea to merge the offices of religion and state.

The Drowned Men give homage to the sea by wearing mottled robes of green, grey, and blue. They frequently clad themselves in sealskin and maintain a wild, unkempt appearance, befitting their status of those that have been claimed from the seas. Priests ritually drink seawater from time to time, believing that the Drowned God gives them everything they need to sustain them.[81] The priests speak with the voice of their god, and thus have considerable political power in the islands. They also have the power to declare a Kingsmoot (albeit rare), which leads to the election of a new king.[82]

During their baptismal ritual (a primitive form of cardiopulmonary resuscitation), the priests recite liturgy. The Drowned Men have no sacred scriptures; everything is passed down by oral history. "Let your servant be born again from the sea, as you were. Bless him with salt, bless him with stone, bless him with steel" (*Clash* 11, Theon I). A man who survives this process is thus consecrated to the Drowned God.

HISTORICAL BACKDROP: SEA DRAGONS OF CHAOS

FANTASY LITERATURE IS saturated with dragons. In Martin's multiverse there are so many Valyrian and Targaryen dragons that the story of Nagga (the sea dragon) is easily overlooked. But make no mistake: when it comes to sea monsters, the Nagga saga blows them out of the agua. The Grey King's slaying of Nagga is a foundational myth for the Iron Islands. It also parallels the foundational myths of several real-world, ancient religions.

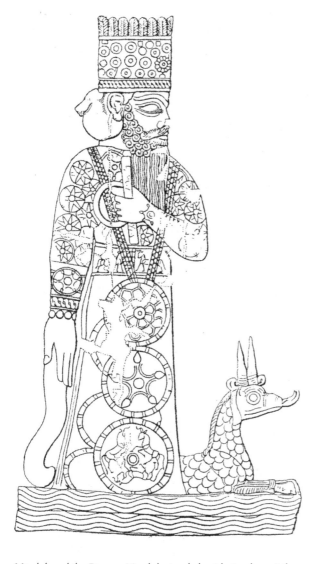

Marduk and the Dragon: Marduk stands beside (and over) the Mushhushshu-dragon. Courtesy of Wikimedia Commons.

Thousands of years before fantasy literature was invented, dragons featured prominently in sacred stories. Long before the flying firedrake of Beowulf, dragons were depicted as creatures of the deep. In the earliest stories about dragons, they did not symbolize power, greed, or magic—at least not primarily. They were symbols of chaos. As we discussed in volume 1, religion is fundamentally opposed to chaos.

In ancient Babylon, the god Marduk was often depicted in human form next to a tamed dragon. It symbolized his dominance over the sea goddess Tiamat and proved that Marduk was powerful enough to bring order to chaos. (Tiamat is variously described as a woman, a creation deity, and a dragon). In this particular story, Marduk is a storm god who arms himself against Tiamat with weapons such as lightning, winds, tornadoes, and a massive flood.[83] He ends up snaring her in his net and puncturing her belly. In some stories, Marduk creates the sky and land from her severed body parts. Because the storm god tames the symbol of chaos, he is sometimes shown with a chaos monster (a dragon) as his pet.

83. In many similar myths, the sea dragon is poisonous. For example, the Japanese water dragon Mizuchi breaths deadly venom. In some myths, the dragon slayer brings healing herbs for anti-venom.

How awesome is it to have a pet dragon? Answer: *it is the awesomest.* Let's just pause to consider how totally awesome it would be to have a pet dragon. . . . The ancient Babylonians thought so too, and esteemed Marduk with praise, honor, and glory. In retrospect, we call this religious mythology. But a better category would be sacred power politics. Historian Robert Miller explains:

> *The basic dragon myth involves
> two characters: the storm god, usually
> connected with the human king of each
> society, and a dragon that represents
> chaos and the sea. The myth details the
> conflict between the two and the victory*

of the storm god, a victory that is some-
times a means of creation. But the
victory also explains why the human
king has the authority to rule, to bring
order to chaos.[84]

As we discussed in chapter 8, the Egyptians used similar political propaganda to support the pharaoh: the pharaoh preserves order (maʾat) and holds back chaos. Life can be unpredictable, so the people need a ruler who has the ear of the dragon-slaying god. From this view, a dragon is "a symbol of something unpredictable, something that is beyond our thinking, just like the sea." Miller continues, "Many societies with dragon imag- ery—India, the Hurrians, Hittites, Israelites—were never seagoing people, so for them the sea was terrifying."

This idea finds its way into the Bible. In Israelite texts, the dragon is called "Leviathan." The Prophet Isaiah writes: "On that day the Lord with his cruel and great and strong sword will punish Leviathan the fleeing serpent, Leviathan the twisting serpent, and he will kill the dragon that is in the sea" (27:1). In this context, slay- ing the dragon makes way for peace in the land.

This story—or some form of it—circulated in several ancient cultures. In fact, the dragon myth is at least as old as the Proto-Indo-European tribes of 10,000 BCE. It is possible that the earliest sky god associated with the weather was Dyēus. While little is known about this mythology, Dyēus seems to have been the prototype for Thor in Norse mythology. Famously, Thor fights the great sea serpent, Jörmungandr. After a series of battles, Thor and Jörmungandr kill each other during the final war of Ragnarök.

84. Robert Miller II, "Dragons in the Bible and Beyond," *The Ancient Near East Today*, www.asor.org, 2018.

Maritime Monstrosity:
Ironborn and other
Blasphemous Fish-frogs
of Nameless Design

Leviathan of "The Last Judgment": Leviathan as imagined by Giacomo Rossignolo (1524–1604 CE) in his fresco "The Last Judgment." Courtesy of Wikimedia Commons.

It is highly likely that some form of this story inspired Martin's Ironborn mythology. Specifically, the story of the Grey King slaying Nagga seems to show several parallels. First, the primary players in the Ironborn myth include a storm god, a sea dragon, and a king who is divinely endorsed. Second, the Grey King slays the dragon, Nagga. The Drowned God then turns Nagga's bones into stone so they can be used to build a house (symbolizing coronation). Third, the victorious dragon slayer is male while the dragon is female. Fourth, and most importantly, the story serves as the foundational myth for a particular tribe.[85]

85. In Ironborn mythology, the Grey King weds a mermaid to father the inhabitants of the Iron Islands. #winning

106

Of course, the primary difference between the stories of Nagga and Tiamat is the location of the "good" deity. In most ancient stories, the storm god is the protagonist. But in Ironborn religion, the Drowned God is allied with the human king. In this fundamental way, the Drowned God is more like "Kumugwe", the undersea god in Pacific Northwest mythology.

Historical Backdrop: Sea Dragons of Chaos

There is no reason to think that Martin had Kumugwe in mind when he invented Ironborn religion. But Kumugwe may be the coolest god ever. Here are ten facts about him:

1. His head is as big as an island.
2. He is the master of seals.
3. His nemesis is Tseiqami, a great bird that makes thunder with its wings and lightning with its eyes.
4. He controls the tides.
5. He sees into the future.
6. He has an octopus bodyguard.
7. He's rich.
8. He eats human eyeballs.
9. If you can find him he might just give you magical powers (or eat your eyeballs).
10. He resides in a house made of living sea lions.[86]

86. Nothing is more gangster than a house made of living sea lions.

Marduk made quick work of the chaos monster. But if he tried to mess with Kumugwe, Marduk would have had his divine ass handed to him.

CHARACTER STUDY:
AERON GREYJOY

BORN THE YOUNGEST son to Quellon Greyjoy, Aeron Greyjoy is best known as a priest of the Drowned God. Aeron is called "Damphair" because he spends so much time in the ocean. His

Maritime Monstrosity:
Ironborn and other
Blasphemous Fish-frogs
of Nameless Design

method of prayer is super-duper damp. It includes allowing the waves wash over him or full submersion (undertow be damned!). He may well be the most devout priest in all of Westeros. Even though Aeron's prayers remain unanswered after months of imprisonment and starvation, he does not doubt. Even when his psychotropic vision reveals the defeat of the Drowned God—impaled and lifeless upon the blades of the Iron Throne—Aeron's faith never wavers (preview chapter of *Winds,* "The Forsaken").

In the face of political and personal turmoil, Damphair concludes that his god is testing his faith. This is both a common refrain in religious circles (medieval and modern) and a popular trope in film. Jesus in *The Last Temptation of Christ,* Nightcrawler in *X-men,* and Sebastião in *Silence* are all examples of religious people who suffer and interpret it as divine testing. These episodes are usually marked by confusion but can include physical suffering too.

The Damphair has a great deal in common with John the Baptist. Both reject creature comforts, both are prophets who commune with nature, both baptize as a purity ritual, and both speak out against corrupt kings (even when there is mortal danger in doing so). The two are so much alike that we can only find one difference: of the two, John the Baptist is the only one who is capable of doubt.[87]

87. Shortly before his death, John the Baptist sends his disciples to Jesus to ask, "Are you the one who is to come, or are we to wait for another?" (Luke 7:19). Such a question would never enter Aeron Greyjoy's mind. (C'mon Damphair, nobody likes a religious know-it-all. Look, even Jesus doubted his fate in the Garden of Gethsemane. Relax, dude.)

John the Baptist's Head: Sometimes you've got to speak your mind to the guy in charge and sometimes it doesn't work out so well. This oil on canvas (ca. 1607) was one of a series of paintings on the subject of John the Baptist by Caravaggio. (Caravaggio was no stranger to dismemberment. The artist once murdered a rival in a botched attempt to castrate him.) Courtesy of Wikimedia Commons.

Character Study:
Aeron Greyjoy

Martin was once asked, "Are the Ironborn's Drowned Men truly drowned?" Martin's reply was direct and concise, "No."[88] *Guess who doesn't give a wet shite about Martin's opinion? That's right: Aeron Greyjoy.* Aeron believes that he drowned to death before washing up on the shore, born anew from the sea. Since then he has been "Damphair the Prophet."

Damphair was abused as child by his brother Euron and spent his young adult years drinking, gambling, and challenging all comers to pissing contests (*Feast* 1, The Prophet). But now he believes that his old life is dead and gone; only the servant of the Drowned God remains. Damphair earnestly believes that he speaks with divine authority.

88. So Spake Martin Archive, July 27, 2008.

89. The full title of the Ironborn king is "King of the Iron Islands and the North, King of Salt and Rock, Son of the Sea Wind, and Lord Reaper of Pyke." This is the titular equivalent to a dude in his fifties who drives his 25 year-old girlfriend around in a red, convertible Corvette.

After Lord Balon "falls" to his death, Damphair prays earnestly for the election of a new Lord Reaper of Pyke.[89] This election takes the form of a "Kingsmoot" (an ancient democratic tradition among the Ironborn). When Euron—his godless and kinslaying brother— wins the Driftwood Crown, Damphair is distraught and decides to use his prophetic voice to create an uprising among the people (*Feast* 19, "The Drowned Man"). *He's already a priest and a prophet, why not become a zealot too?*

After praying and soaking, Damphair receives a divine endorsement for the royal duo of Victarion (his other brother) and Asha (his niece). He is confident that the marriage of these two will make for an ideal royal couple. Before he can begin his religious revolution, however, Euron captures him and sets sail for the Shield Islands. Damphair is chained, deprived of food and sunlight, subdued into a hallucinogenic state, and forced to witness torture. Eventually, he's strapped to the bow of Euron's ship as a living figurehead. Even so, his faith doesn't waver. He trusts that he will soon be in the watery halls of his god.

All considered, we think John the Baptist had the preferable outcome.

FAN THEORY FUN:
THE MERLING KING

VARYS IS A *delightful* character. Intelligent, cunning, and self-made, he's one of the few people who can best Littlefinger in a scheme-off, best Tyrion in a banter-off, or best Theon in a penis-off. That said, Varys plays the game of thrones with metaphorical gonads of Valyrian steel.

Varys is the odd duck in our cast of characters. He is low born, yet serves a lord's position. He is a foreigner to Westeros, and one who has lost his literal gonads in a world where being seen as anything less than a man is a sign of weakness. As a result of his eunuchood, he is viewed by almost everyone as socially, legally, and biologically inferior. Moreover, his inability to pass his success to progeny renders moot all consideration of legacy.

Fan Theory Fun:
The Merling King

This fascinating cocktail of oddity makes us wonder, *just who in the hell's side is he on, and what the hell is he up to? What motivates him, and why?* Varys will always insist that his loyalties are to the realm. But isn't this exactly what a guy with super-genius ulterior motives would say?

At this point you're no doubt wondering, "Okay, Varys is cool. But he is connected to the Ironborn, *how?*" And the truth is, fancy-lad reader, you've got us. We can see that you've clearly bought into the "approved narrative" of Varys, and that's fine. It's probably safer for you that way. Best to let old Varys' motives, schemes and ambitions remain a mystery because there are people out there who don't want us to ask big questions. Big questions like, what if the situation is even more complicated than just the inscrutable desires of the human heart? What if Varys *isn't* human but is in fact a merman sent from the Narrow Sea as the vanguard of an inhuman invasion force?[90] Once you open your mind to accept this essential truth, Varys' motives become clear as day, as does his placement in this no-nonsense-nautical chapter.[91]

Mermen and Mermaids are definitely a thing in Westeros. Collectively known as merlings, they are well established in legend and rumor. They are more promi-

90. This theory was pioneered by "Nightflyer" at The Forum of Ice and Fire, May 27, 2008.

91. We haven't lost our minds. We realize that this has as much chance of being true as the pirate Salladhor Saan has of sitting the Iron Throne. But it is a really fun example of how you can twist a text into crazy balloon animal shapes with a little bit of gumption. It's not like the Man made us put in this footnote so you can live in your safe bubble where you don't have to fear a life of subjugation to fish people. That would be *ridiculous.*

nent in coastal areas and with sea faring cultures such as the Iron Islanders, but even the most ignorant landlubber who's ever lubbed a land has at least heard of them. The Manderlys of White Harbor feature a merling as their house sigil (*Thrones* 55, Catelyn VIII). The Merling King is among the deities that the Faceless Men honor with a statue in their House of Black and White (*Feast* 22, Arya II). At least one maester from the Iron Islands suggests that some culture of intelligent sea folk is the true origin of the Ironborn religion (*World*, "The Reach: Oldtown").

Fan Theory Fun:
The Merling King

Merlings are assumed to be mythological beings, just like krakens, grumkins, snarks, mammoths, giants, white walkers, children of the forest, and Fisher Queens.[92] In the beginning of the series, almost any maester of the Citadel would tell you that none of these could possibly be real. And yet as we draw near to the end of the series, we've come face to face with half of these fantastic beasts. Are we so sure merlings can't live hidden in the depths? Or, more to the point, perhaps one of them is hidden in plain view.

92. One of the earliest societies in the legends of Essos was called the "Fisher Queens." They are not associated with merling mythology, but they seemingly ruled from floating cities in the Silver Sea. In Sarnor legends, the Fisher Queens were a wise, beneficent folk (perhaps a nod to the Atlantis myth?) who were favored by the gods.

What do we really know about Varys, anyway? He's not a point-of-view character in the novels, so we never get a glimpse of his internal thoughts or feelings, fishy as they might be. We know he's bald, a eunuch, and good with disguises (*Game* 30, Eddard VII; *Storm* 12, Tyrion II). His smile is frequently described as slimy (*Clash* 8, Tyrion II). He's described as heavy and habitually wears full body robes that obscure his lower half.

These features could well describe a secret merling disguised to live as a common biped. Of course his smile is slimy! Who knows if he even has teeth? He might not have a human penis, sure, but not because he's emasculated. He's hung like a mackerel![93] Even a cursory look under those robes would quickly blow his cover. But as a

93. And you know what they say about mackerel. Big fins? Big gondopodium.

94. Counter point: *The Little
Mermaid, Splash,* and *Creature from
the Black Lagoon* (e.g.) fairly teem
with randy fish folk wanting to climb
homo sapien like a tree, and vice versa. Still, we think it's safe to assume
that fish-on-person attraction would
be the exception rather than the rule.
And just so that this footnote isn't
misconstrued to paint us as unrepen-
tant ichthyophobes as the seas rise
and fish people inherit the earth, we
hasten to add that if carp copulation
is the outcome of consenting parties,
it is none of our business.

merling, he is as sexually attractive to us as we would be to a carp.[94] He promotes the story of the warlock severing his root and stem to discourage interest in his body and explain his apparent complete lack of sexual appetite.

Varys' bulk combined with flowing robes could very well hide the fact that there is something fishy going on with his lower half. We've never seen his feet. Those robes and silk slippers could hide any unsightly fins or scales.

Varys sleeps on a solid slab of stone, which he blames on a bad back. Sure, maybe his sleep number is 100, but a *stone slab?* And we later find out that this bed is a ruse! It's a giant trap door that covers access to the twisted warren of secret tunnels allowing him to travel through the Red Keep unseen and unheard (*Storm* 12, Tyrion 11).

If his bed is a facade, we demand to know: where does he *really* sleep? Consider this early clue: Arya discovers Varys creeping around in subterranean tunnels with Illyrio as they conspire to destabilize the Baratheon regime (*Game* 32, Arya III; S01E05, "The Wolf and the Lion"). In the books they're described as dripping with water, and Arya sees the pair pop out of secret passage concealed by a well. How convenient that Varys' fake bed connects directly to a source of water! Arya is able to follow these tunnels, which lead to a sewer, which in turn flows into a river, and then into the ocean (a.k.a. Varys' *actual home*).

Speaking of Varys' tunnel-buddy, Illyrio, he's another habitually robed chonk. Don't look now, but we may have a merling conspiracy, which implies other conspirators! What about Lord Manderly of White Harbor? Oh, he's fully human. A fully human fat man, with a taste for human flesh (*Dance* 37, The Prince of Winterfell), who has a *merling* for his house's sigil. Wake up, sheeple!

Still not convinced? An exchange between Varys and Tyrion is telling. When Tyrion threatens to throw Varys into the sea, Varys warns him, "You may be disappointed in the result. The storms come and go, the waves crash overhead, and I keep on paddling" (*Clash* 8, Tyrion II; *Thrones* S02E02, "The Night Lands"). Don't think for a moment that this is an innocent maritime metaphor. This is exactly what our merling overlords would have us believe.

We're quite certain that Tyrion would be *disappointed* to see Varys transform into a human jet ski and summon his merling army to destroy King's Landing.

Let's also consider Varys' main antagonist, Petyr Baelish (seemingly so). Littlefinger claims to have power over Varys (*Game* 20, Eddard IV), boasting "I hold the man's balls in the palm of my hand. Or would if he was a man or had balls."

What could Lord Baelish possibly have over Varys? Perhaps his super-secret identity? After all, Littlefinger's personal vessel (*Storm* 61, Sansa V) is called "The Merling King." Perhaps this is a subtle jab at his chief political rival?

We started down this dark path by wondering about Varys' endgame. Indeed it is among the favorite time-wasting topics on our favorite fan forums. Many readers assume that Varys isn't the altruistic realm-lover that he (or she[95]) claims to be. It is possible that his endgame is a long-con whereby he undermines Targaryen rule to the point of exile and then flips Westeros back to a once-great ruling class. Or, speaking more generally, there's a vague notion that he's working with Illyrio to put a Targaryen back on the Iron Throne,

Fan Theory Fun:
The Merling King

95. Yes, we said "she." Some fans suspect that Varys is Illyrio's wife. See "Varys is a Woman" by Quite Isle at A Forum of Ice and Fire, Oct. 7, 2012.

because ... reasons. It's all very nebulous, and no one is quite sure where this is going, or why.

However, one thing is clear. Varys and Illyrio have armed Dany with dragons, putting them firmly on Team Fire in the wars to come. This is, of course, *A Song of Ice and Fire*. What do you get when you combine fire and ice? *Water*. Imagine *(it's easy if you try)* an army of dragons that brings an eternal summer, melting the icy Wall and thawing the Lands of Always Winter. The waters will inevitably rise, providing *Lebensraum* for the merlings' aggressive expansion. The resulting refugee crisis and destabilized realms will lead to a veritable bounty of dead humans for the flesh-hungry merlings to feast upon.

In this dark future only a few high places remain where the rule of men holds sway: places like the Vale, with its mountain stronghold, the Eyrie. Say, who is currently the Lord Protector of the Vale? Oh, that's right...
Littlefinger, the Merling King!

BIRD'S-EYE VIEW: ELDRITCH APOCALYPSE

A S A NOVELIST, Martin has an oceanic capacity for dark themes and horrific tension. He's also a fan of comical farce. In homage to the latter, *A Song of Ice and Fire* is overflowing with winks and nods to characters in other novels and television. When asked if the characters Lharys, Kurleket, and Mohor (*Game* 31, Tyrion IV) were tips of the hat to "The Three Stooges" (Larry, Curly, and Moe) Martin replied,

> *The Three Stooges? In my book? C'mon, you've got to be kidding. Would I do something like that? That's a very tense chapter, charged with menace,*

Maritime Monstrosity: Ironborn and other Blasphemous Fish-frogs of Nameless Design

what are you laughing for? If I were
to insist that the names were purely a
coincidence, you'd buy it, wouldn't you?
Okay, okay, what can I say? Guilty as
charged. I don't know what came over
me. I'm not even that big a Stooges
fan . . . there are indeed more "hidden
characters," though I prefer to think of
them as "homages" or "a tip of the hat."
Writers, mostly—fantasists or histori-
cal novelists whose names I borrow for
background characters.[96]

Bird's-Eye View:
Eldritch Apocalypse

96. So Spake Martin Archive, Mar. 10, 2006.

The keen-eyed reader will, therefore, find winks and nods to external stories throughout Martin's writing. In one of his more intriguing homages, Martin has drawn from the horror fiction of H. P. Lovecraft (1890–1937), specifically from his novella, *The Shadow Over Innsmouth.* This story is now famous for its squid-faced gods and the occult rituals used to worship them. They are called the "Deep Ones," they are utterly evil, and they're among us as human-fish hybrids!

In the Lovecraft story, an investigator discovers a cult that resides in the town of Innsmouth, Massachusetts. The cult, called the Esoteric Order of Dagon,[97] is entangled with the Deep Ones in two deeply disturbing ways: (1) they offer human sacrifices in exchange for jewelry and fish, and (2) they breed with their fishy overlords to produce new fishy progeny (think "The Shape of Water" with heavy doses of psychedelic tentacles and supernatural yuck).

It was only a matter of time before a perceptive reader of Lovecraft discovered that Martin was leaving clues.[98] Most of these clues came from Martin's world-

97. Dagon (a fish deity) is sometimes associated with Canaanite worship.

98. What follows began as a fan theory. But unlike many of its peers, which can be little more than tinfoil folded together by fevered minds, this one was crafted from Valyrian tinfoil, fortified with the dragon-fire of logic and plausibility. Credit goes to one Emmitt Booth, who goes by the handle @PoorQuentyn on Twitter and Tumblr. Booth provided a literary hypothesis and then confirmed his theory with observations made in both *The World of Ice & Fire* and the preview chapter of *Winds* titled "The Forsaken."

99. On the screen, Euron is little more than comic relief. In the dark ideations of Martin, he is a human sacrificing, mass murdering, kinslaying, serial rapist. Euron makes other Iron Islanders look like the guest list of the Catalina Wine Mixer.

building of the crownlands and the Iron Islands (two cultures that look to be on a collision course). Here is the sample platter: a reference to "Deep Ones," a reference to a Lord Dagon, rumors of human-fish hybrids, some seriously weird mineralogy, and the unspeakable evil that is Euron Greyjoy.[99]

This has become known as the "Eldritch Apocalypse". The proponents of this theory argue that the clues add up to more than mere hat tips. If super fans like Emmitt Booth are correct, the Lovecraftian mythos is the key to unlocking the aims of Euron Greyjoy who is poised to invade Oldtown. One clear echo to Lovecraft can be heard in the prophecy of a red priest named Moqorro. In his visions he sees a "tall and twisted thing with one black eye and ten long arms, sailing on a sea of blood" (*Dance* 33, Tyrion VIII). This description seems to echo Lovecraft's Cthulhu, a giant, humanoid, squid-headed monster with batwings.

A second Lovecraft hat tip is found in Martin's *The World of Ice & Fire*. Maester Theron from the Iron Islands mentions Deep Ones. Theron calls them a "queer, misshapen race of half men sired by creatures of the salt seas upon human women. These Deep Ones, as he names them, are the seed from which our legends of merlings have grown, he argues, whilst their terrible fathers are the truth behind the Drowned God of the Ironborn" (*World,* "The Reach: Oldtown"). Building from these clear allusions, several other Martin-Lovecraft parallels become clear.

Now, if you're not a Lovecraft aficionado, this may sound outlandish. But the Eldritch Apocalypse picked up new momentum when Martin released a *Winds* chapter titled "The Forsaken." Here we get a better glimpse of Euron from Damphair's point of view.

Damphair is imprisoned by his brother Euron, who forces him to ingest a hallucinogenic. While in the throes of the substance, he has powerful visions of Euron sitting on a throne of skulls. Then he sits on the Iron Throne, impaled gods hanging from it's swords. Damphair envisions Euron laughing over the dead corpses of the gods of Westeros and Essos—including the Ironborn's own Drowned God. Here we get a direct allusion to Lovecraft's Cthulhu: "He seemed more squid than man, a monster fathered by a kraken of the deep, his face a mass of writhing tentacles" (*Winds*, "The Forsaken").

Bird's-Eye View:
Eldritch Apocalypse

In addition to this vision, Euron is busy performing thousands of blood sacrifices and is specifically interested in sacrificing the priests of other religions. All this is preparation for his invasion of Oldtown.[100] It seems highly likely that Euron is worshipping some sort of deep-sea deity, one that isn't standard among the Ironborn.

If indeed Martin has the Lovecraftian Deep Ones in mind, these would be creatures of immense power.[101] It might also be helpful to know that in Lovecraft's universe, humans can be Deep Ones in disguise (sometimes without knowing it). This usually involves the discovery that your mother was a human and your father was a little bit froggy. As luck would have it, this kind of thing happens in Martin's world too.

Ready?

There are legendary creatures rumored to live at Crackclaw Point, a peninsula in the crownlands. These creatures, called "squishers," are said to resemble humans, but with larger heads, scaly skin, webbed fingers and toes, and needle sharp teeth (*Feast* 20, Brienne IV). They are said to prey on children, eating the boys and saving the girls to breed more squishers (this describes

100. In preparation for Euron's invasion, some of the Hightowers lock themselves in their famous Tower (Lord Leyton chief among them), consulting books of spells to stop the encroaching fleet of Euron Greyjoy. Locals ponder if Leyton is trying to "raise an army from the deeps" (*Feast* 45, Samwell V).

101. Hightower's lowest level is an intricate fortress of ancient tunnels (*World*, "The Reach: Oldtown").

the parallel revelation at Innsmouth, Massachusetts perfectly). Nearby, House Borrell has a genetic quirk that gives them webbed fingers (*Dance* 9, Davos 1). They call this "the Mark."

In short, there is something fishy going on near the coastal regions of the crownlands and the Iron Islands. Two questions remain: what connects these two regions, and why is Euron hell-bent on sacking Oldtown?

We might have an answer to the first question. The Seastone Chair (on Pyke) appears to be made of the same mineralogical substance as the foundation of Hightower (in Oldtown).[102] This "stone" of unknown origin is described as oily and black. Most maesters have no explanation for the origin of these structures that predate all known human cultures.[103] The only hint of a theory comes from a discredited maester named Theron from the Ironborn. Maester Theron argues that the chair and foundation were both built by the Deep Ones, who might even predate the Children of the Forest.

So why is Euron hell-bent on sacking Oldtown? Our favorite Lovecraft conspiracy theorist, Mr. Booth believes that Euron will sacrifice his own fleet and the fleet defending Oldtown in order to raise a massive army of the dead. He will merge with an evil unnamed god that Euron discovered in his travels to the haunted seas of Old Valyria. The method for this supernatural merger remain vague. Maybe it involves some blood magic he's learned at the feet of the Three Eyed Crow, or in the classes of Marwyn the Mage (one of the few maesters who studies magic). He's basically Rasputin from *Hellboy,* if Rasputin aspired to acquire face-tentacles.[104]

Proponents of the Eldritch Apocalypse theory suggest that Euron will use a blood magic boost to defeat the Others and claim the world for himself, or to join

102. Hightower's lowest level is an intricate fortress of ancient tunnels. This fortress connects it to the Greyjoy's kraken-shaped throne. Both seem to be made of an oily, black stone that remains a mystery to the maesters (*World*, "The Reach: Oldtown").

103. Lovecraft writes this of a similar stone sculpture related to the Deep Ones: "It's very material was a mystery; for the soapy, greenish-black stone with its golden or iridescent flecks and striations resembled nothing familiar to geology or mineralogy." Part II of "The Call of Cthulhu," *Weird Tales,* 1928.

104. We mean that Euron is Rasputin, not Emmitt Booth. We're sure that Mr. Booth is a fine, upstanding citizen with no face-tentacles whatsoever.

his undead and otherworldly strength to the Others, betraying all mankind for personal power.

Regardless of how this ends up fitting into the final events of *A Song of Ice and Fire,* it's clear that Martin definitely baked some Lovecraftian salt into the soufflé. It remains to be seen whether the Deep Ones will become a major plot point or if they are merely an homage, much like his nods to *Frankenstein*, *Dracula*, and the *Three Stooges*.

Bird's-Eye View:
Eldritch Apocalypse

Death in Many Faces

12

Death would not be called bad, O people, if one knew how to die truly.

— GURU NANAK

Distinctive Elements

- monotheistic universalism
- self-emptying as life ethic
- cultural appropriation
- ninja-level sneakiness

Key Adherents

- a girl is no one
- a man is no one

TRAVEL GUIDE

ONCE HIDDEN FROM outsiders and shrouded by mystery, the Secret City of Braavos is now open for tourism. This Braavosi channel of islands has everything a honeymoon should: fog, marshland, rigid bankers, a stinking fish market, a shouting statue, shape-shifting spies, freezing rain, and assassins. And what honeymoon hideaway would be complete without the option for euthanasia?

Take your love affair to the next level with a *Romeo and Juliet* ending. The House of Black and White is perfect for destination weddings. It will provide a priestly accomplice, a cavernous sanctuary, and an unhealthy dose of poison. The blind acolytes will—at no extra charge!—ritually prepare your body for blood magic. Nothing says romance like a ninja in a Leatherface mask.

Not into blood-magic fueled suicide? Honeymoons don't have to be all fun and games. Make your nuptial celebration more practical by visiting the Iron Bank. Their tall, gaunt loan specialists can help you with a home purchase. Or if you're aiming higher, you and your new spouse can apply for world-conquest funding. Why settle for a home when you can use that nest egg to buy an army? It's never too soon to invest in the future. Make your honeymoon a holiday that works for you!

Death in Many Faces: Arya, Underfoot, Arry, Boy, Girl, Cat, Blind Beth, and Mercy

DEEP DIVE: FROM MAGMA TO DOGMA

ARYA AND THE Hound are unhappily tripping through the countryside doing Bonnie and Clyde things. While Sandor is drinking the pain away, Arya is fast becoming a Faceless-Men acolyte. She may not know it yet but she's learning to understand, meditate on, maybe even worship death. It makes her one of Martin's most compelling personalities and yet we can't help but wonder if we're witnessing a *Breaking Bad* character spiral.

Sandor, of course, isn't breaking bad; he's broken. One of the first things Arya learns about the Hound is that he's a killer. Worse, he's killed her friend on Joffrey's orders (*Game* 16, Eddard III). Mycah was innocent, Joffrey a budding psychopath, and Sandor didn't care. Legally speaking, the Hound does what the prince commands. Morally speaking, he just enjoys killing. Long after he's left Joffrey's court, he still enjoys killing. Arya, on the other hand, is complicated. She genuinely hates the Hound but she's starting to admire him. She knows that murdering the innocent is wrong. She also has a heart full of vengeance. If Arya could just learn to be more like Sandor, she might be able to kill a few fools that need killing.

Deep Dive: From Magma to Dogma

One of Martin's most bewitching talents is the ability to take a murderer like Sandor and set him on a redemptive path. Arya makes this possible. Sandor needs Arya to imagine himself as something more than Joffrey's dog or his brother's mutton chop. Somewhere inside him is empathy and compassion but he needs Arya to help him explore how these aspects will play out in the real world. It's probably safe to say that Sandor becomes a bit more like Arya and Arya becomes a bit more like Sandor. If so, our favorite Stark child is on a dark path.

Beatrix Kiddo (*Kill Bill: vol. 2*) tells us that people who have lost their father will sometimes collect father figures. This is certainly true of Arya, who finds a series of mentors along her way. Each mentor teaches her something about death. Jon Snow teaches her the first rule of swordplay, "stick 'em with the pointy end." Syrio Forel introduces her to Braavosi culture and the "water dance." Yoren teaches Arya to say the names on her kill list like a prayer (show only).[105] Jaqen H'ghar points her toward Faceless-Men theology. Tywin teaches her cunning and wartime strategy (show only). Sandor teaches her how to kill and that some men relish it. Each of these is a stepping stone on her path to becoming the most dangerous assassin in Westeros. But in each case, Arya takes what she needs from her mentor and moves on. She never stays with a mentor long enough to become fully devoted.

Arya's longest and most immersive apprenticeship is in the House of Black and White. Among the worship-

105. On screen, Yoren tells the story about the man who killed his brother. He repeats the killer's name (Willem) every night like a prayer (S02E03, "What is Dead May Never Die"). Martin's original story was that Arya invented the prayer on her own. In *Clash*, Arya recalls how she prayed with her mother in Winterfell. Eventually, "her names were the only prayers she cared to remember" (*Clash* 26, Arya VI).

pers of the Many-Faced God she becomes a novice and a blind acolyte. Indeed she is quickly acquiring the skills and trade of a Faceless Man. This stage of her journey places her among an elite society of assassins within the larger system of worship. In order to advance in the temple system, the novice must undergo a long and painful process of identity loss. Arya must convince her priest that she truly believes she is "no one." We get the sense that Arya is truly devoted to the temple and maybe even the God worshipped by the society. But she never fully surrenders her identity.

Real-world Analogs to Faceless Theology

Worship of the Many-Faced God incorporates several sacred myths into an amalgam of beliefs. Priests of the House of Black and White teach that their God is represented by the Stranger of Westeros, the Black Goat of Qohor, the Lion of Night in Yi Ti, etc. Because death is part of the human experience, the god of death wears many faces. In keeping with this belief, the temple merges various symbols, statues, altars, and weirwood into a museum of cultural appropriation.

It makes sense, then, that Martin borrows from several real-world religious traditions to invent this system of worship. Like Buddhism, it originates out of a concern for suffering and emphasizes self-emptying. Like Judaism, its hub is a singular temple (rather than many) and it originates from a community of freed slaves. Like Sikhism, it believes in the unity of God and promotes ridding oneself of ego. Like the Hindu concept

126

of "brahman, the divine," it holds that the names of the gods are less important that their ultimate singularity. Like Santa Muerte worship,[106] it syncs up with other religions and reveres Death. Like the Italian mafia, it can "take care of that thing" for you.[107]

Deep Dive: From Magma to Dogma

In learning the temple's doctrine, Arya must unlearn her own ego. Hiding her blade is the first clue that Arya does not intend to surrender fully (*Feast* 22, Arya II / S05E03, "High Sparrow"). She is willing to give up all other personal items but she intends to retrieve Needle. The blade is a link to her childhood at Winterfell, to Jon Snow, and to the first steps of her journey. Second, Arya continues to dream of being a wolf. She maintains her spiritual connection to Nymeria even while in Braavos (book only).[108] Third, Arya doesn't forget the names on her kill list. In other words, she has her own private death prayer that isn't mediated by the priests. When interrogated in the temple, she tries to keep her identity and motives hidden but her face gives her away. Her nameless mentor observes, "You have the eyes of a wolf and a taste for blood." In order to preserve her lie, she says nothing and meditates on her personal prayer (*Dance* 64, "The Ugly Little Girl").

This last point is crucial for understanding the distance between Arya and the priests of the Many-Faced God. They emerged from a slave and then refugee population from the Valyrian Freehold. They trace their spiritual heritage to the first Faceless Man, a slave who worked alongside many other slaves mining for volcanic ore in hellish conditions. According to legend, the first Faceless man formed a single spiritual community from many cultures living in the volcanic mines. Therein, he

106. You may recall that the Salamanca cousins from *Breaking Bad* were devout worshippers. They begin their mission to kill Walter White by crawling a mile to a Santa Muerte shrine in *very* expensive suits. While we have not met many actual devotees, we imagine that those who venerate Our Lady of Death have a better sense of stewardship of high-end fashion.

107. Some early manuscripts translate *valar dohaeris* as "hey, *fuhgeddaboudit.*"

108. For more on this, see chapter 9: "Night Gathers." Arya's supernatural connection to her direwolf is absent in the show. This makes it somewhat surprising to see her stumble upon Nymeria in season seven (S07E02, "Stormborn"). Perhaps this is a hint that the direwolf will play a role in the conclusion of Arya's part of the *Song*?

preached the essential oneness of God. *In other words, his dogma began in magma.*

From the outset, the Faceless Men are a collective; their individual identities are less important than the group. Even individual prayers directed to various gods of various names—if understood truly—are spoken in service to the one God. Once they escaped their captors and established a unified belief system, their doctrine about death became clear: it ought to function as a merciful end to suffering.

In case it isn't clear, Arya's interest in death is not motivated by mercy. Not only does Arya maintain her individualistic prayer (her kill list), she remains personally motivated by vengeance.

Now this is where the morality gets a bit gray in the House of Black and White. From a pro-Faceless view, the temple provides a place to end suffering. The priests offer their "gift" to those ravaged by disease and in unbearable pain. To those who need it, the temple is a place to end their suffering peacefully and say goodbye to loved ones. It is also a place for travelers to pray to their various gods away from home.

From an anti-Faceless view, the secret society is little more than a *John Wick* underground. The Faceless Men are in the murder-for-hire business. The cost is commensurate with the supposed value of the target. Does this society serve the Many-Faced God or the contents of Iron Bank (also located in Braavos)? Taking this line a step further: all of the corpses acquired in the temple become new faces for their disguises. They need those new faces to create their blood-magic masks, which leads to the question: *Does the House of Black and White really adhere to its own dogma?*[109]

Death in Many Faces: Arya, Underfoot, Arry, Boy, Girl, Cat, Blind Beth, and Mercy

109. One answer to this is that the Faceless Men are the arbiters of the Faceless God and they really, *really* mean it when they say, "All men must serve." *Valar dohaeris* isn't optional; it's a requirement. Jacking people's faces to continue their mission is thus for the greater good. If the deity needs your face, your face gets got. Ultimately, it will be up to audiences to decide whether these super-sacred assassins are really interested in the general well-being of society.

Arya is driven by her many vendettas and her growing taste for blood. We hope that she finds peace, balance, and stability before she spirals into Walter White territory. But we can't blame her for choosing her own identity over and against the egoless requirements of an acolyte.

Deep Dive: From Magma to Dogma

Hildegard of Bingen: While Arya's status as a female acolyte might seem anachronistic, medieval orders sometimes included prominent females. One of the most prominent was Hildegard of Bingen (1098–1179). She founded the monasteries of Rupertsberg and Eibingen and wrote on theology, philosophy, the natural sciences, etc. The above image is an illumination from her Book of Divine Works, titled "Universal Man." Courtesy of Wikimedia Commons.

HISTORICAL BACKDROP: DEATH COINS

Death in Many Faces:
Arya, Underfoot,
Arry, Boy, Girl, Cat,
Blind Beth, and Mercy

THE RELATIONSHIP BETWEEN death rituals and coinage is at least as old as the Greeks. But, as always, every good funerary-rite story begins in Egypt. The afterlife, it was believed, required many of the same resources that people used during life: gold, servants, furniture, etc. For the wealthy, death was a huge hassle; not only were you dead, but you had to arrange to have your stuff moved.

Wealthy Egyptians were often buried with a boat or multiple boats. Their purpose is a matter of debate but one prominent theory is that a boat was required to carry the deceased to the afterlife. Gold, food, boats, and other creature comforts are commonly found at wealthy Egyptian burial sites.[110]

110. Coins were not invented before the 8th century BCE and weren't commonly traded until the 5th century.

Greek Obol: An example of a coin used as "Charon's Obol" minted between the 5th and 1st centuries BCE. This coin is probably too thin for use as currency and coins like it are often found in burial sites. Courtesy of cngcoins.com via Wikimedia Commons.

Alongside the material evidence from archeological digs, Egyptian mythology includes at least two ferrymen who taxied people to the afterlife. One was named Mahaf; another was named Kherty. Kherty may have been the inspiration for the Greek ferryman for the dead, named Kharon (or Charon). In the Greek adaptation of this myth, the ferryman required payment. If you wanted to get to the realm of Hades (rather than wander the river banks bodiless) you'd need to get your relatives to bury you with a coin in your mouth. Kharon would take the coin—called the "obol"—as boat fare.

As Christianity spread in later centuries, ideas about the afterlife evolved and Kharon's obol rituals diminished in popularity. But death coins continued to play a part in funerary rites. Specifically, coins were repurposed to hold shut the eyelids of the deceased.

Archeological evidence suggests that this custom wasn't popular until the Middle Ages. The ritual of shutting the eyes of the dead is very ancient, however, and mentioned in Genesis 46:4, ". . . and Joseph's own hand shall close your eyes." In Jewish tradition, broken pottery was sometimes used to cover the eyes of the dead, so it is possible that Christianity adapted the coin-on-eye trick from their Abrahamic siblings.[111] If so, eye coinage isn't there to pay the ferryman; the coins are just paperweights for eyelids in the same way that stones were used to cover Tywin's dead-mackerel eyes (S05E01, "The Wars to Come"). Starting around the 12th century, wealthy Europeans would sometimes mint funerary coins to commemorate the dead. These were simply collected in their honor.

111. In seems that the internet is collectively convinced that coins over eyes at funerals is borrowed from Kharon's obol. But the evidence for this is slim (hence the guesswork). The practice may in fact stem from the belief that evil spirits could enter the dead through open eyes. That said, there seems to be no clear consensus among archeologists on the ideology behind the ritual.

Death in Many Faces:
Arya, Underfoot,
Arry, Boy, Girl, Cat,
Blind Beth, and Mercy

Frederick's Funerary Coin: To commemorate the death of John Frederick, Duke of Brunswick-Lüneburg (1679), this coin was minted in his honor. On one side Death is depicted as a skeleton; on the other are his initials "JF." Courtesy of the National Numismatic Collection; National Museum of American History via Wikimedia Commons.

The coin given to Arya by Jaqen (a.k.a. "what's his face") probably reflects a combination of funerary coin practice and secret society tokens. For example, during the Taiping uprising in China (1850–1864) a secret society called the Tiandihui emerged. Members would carry coins and reveal them to receive benefits from other members or those sympathetic to the society. This ritual is still practiced in many modern military units that use "challenge coins" to prove their membership. The benefit is often simply a free drink from their comrades in arms.

When Arya pays the Braavosi captain to take her across the Narrow Sea, she uses a coin that is known to represent the Faceless Men (*Storm* 74, Arya XIII). The captain—almost in awe of the coin—honors Arya with a cabin. The coin is iron with writing (she cannot read) on one side and a face (with no features) on the other. She is instructed by Jaqen to give the coin to any man from Braavos and say *valar morghulis* (words she does not understand). When she does, she is boated to the House of Black and White. All considered, this iron coin is associated with death, a secret society, and probably echoes the myth of Kharon's boat fare. Arya literally pays the ferryman to boat her to the temple of death.

CHARACTER STUDY:
WHAT'S HIS FACE

ANY STUDY OF Jaqen H'ghar must acknowledge that his name, backstory, and beliefs are suspect. (We know, bad start. But it gets better.) Does "Jaqen H'ghar" allow Arya a peek into his interior? Is this an identity that an opaque Faceless Man temporarily assumed to influence Arya? Or is the right answer simply that *a man is no one*? Each of these answers has its merits. Because Jaqen H'ghar is a dubious identity, we'll stick to how he appears in the story from Arya's perspective and as a literary type.

Jaqen appears to be from Lorath, an island city near Braavos. The god worshipped there is Boash and those who follow Boash believe that all life is precious. This includes animal life, so they promote a vegetarian diet. The second key distinctive of the Lorathi is their speech. To engender humility, the language avoids first-person, singular pronouns (*World*, "Lorath"). Jaqen reflects this as he refers to himself as "a man" rather than "I" or "me." Arya first encounters him as polite and humble in keeping with the Lorathi reputation.

Such egoless values might fit well within the House of Black and White where personal identity is suppressed. But we wonder, would a good Lorathi seek training as an assassin for the Many-Faced God? *Don't Lorathi value all living creatures?* While Arya experiences him as a man from Lorath, it is possible that Jaqen's persona is a mask made from a deceased Lorathi.

133

112. Later Jaqen swears an oath to Arya and seems to emphasize R'hllor: "By all the gods of sea and air, and even him of fire, I swear it" (*Clash* 47, Arya IX).

To complicate matters further, Jaqen appears to serve the "Red God," seemingly a reference to R'hllor. He and two other prisoners are in danger of burning to death, locked in a wagon engulfed in flames. Arya brings him an axe to break free (*Clash* 14, Arya IV). Once they are both at Harrenhal, Jaqen claims that three lives were stolen from the Red God and therefore three lives are now owed (*Clash* 30, Arya VII / S02E05, "The Ghost of Harrenhal"). Assuming that Jaqen is accurately reflecting Faceless theology, this may be a nod to the way he and his two companions would have died—*by fire*. Because the Many-Faced God sometimes wears the mask of the Red God, death by fire is associated with the divine veneer.[112] But the problem with this theory is that the three people who die by Jaqen's hands at Harrenhal—those who are *owed* to the Red God—do not die by fire. In other words, Jaqen kills them in other ways. So the reference to the Red God remains awkward and in the end reveals very little about the beliefs of the Faceless Men.

Much of Arya's storyline at Harrenhal is driven by her encounter with Jaqen. Because she has saved three lives from the flames, Jaqen tells her she must choose three people to die. *You know, because every 10 year-old should be in charge of a few human sacrifices.* Simply put, she now has her own personal assassin who will hit three targets of her choosing. Arya chooses two names from her list: Weese and Chiswyck (for show fans, the Tickler and Ser Amory Lorch). Her third name (initially) is Jaqen H'ghar. Arya has bigger plans in mind, but in that moment, she stuns Jaqen with her choice.

From Arya's perspective Jaqen is more distressed by hearing his name than he was when engulfed in flames. Eventually she lets him off the hook as he promises to kill a number of guards and help her escape Harrenhal.

Before he leaves her service, the assassin—in a sense—kills Jaqen H'ghar by simply casting off this identity. He changes his face and eliminates the person he used to be (*Clash* 47, Arya IX; S02E10, "Valar Morghulis"). It is possible that the same assassin turns up in the Citadel to kill Pate and take his identity.[113]

For all of the mystery that surrounds Jaqen, he functions almost as a *jinni (or djinni)* of folk literature. In popular fantasy—from which Martin borrows from time to time—the genie gives Aladdin three wishes.[114] In folklore, *jinn* are more like simple spirits, creatures who are concealed from the senses. The root word *jnn* (or *jann*) literally means "to conceal." In Islamic lore, *jinn* are thought to be creatures born of fire.[115] More importantly, in keeping with popular fantasy, Jaqen offers three wishes.

Famously, Aladdin encounters the *jinni* by polishing a magic lamp. In Arya's story, Martin uses the metaphor of "polishing" right before Arya's first kill-list prayer. "Arya watched and listened and polished her hates the way Gendry had once polished his horned helm" (*Clash* 26, Arya VI). Jaqen H'ghar shows up soon after to answer her prayer, at least in part. Finally, when children imagine having three wishes, inevitably they will try to figure out a way to get more wishes. This is exactly what Arya does. She tricks Jaqen into giving her more lives than he was initially willing to give.

In sum, Arya's relationship with Jaqen is born in fire. He becomes indebted to her when she releases him, he must give her three desires of heart, he is eventually tricked into giving her more, and he departs by concealing his identity. No, Jaqen's not literally a genie. But he functions as a literary genie for Arya's peculiar

113. The man was described as "the Alchemist." His appearance matched the man that left Arya's service (*Feast*, "Prologue"). This man seems to have acquired the Archmaester's key from Pate and has (perhaps) stayed at the Citadel until Sam Tarley arrives. Sam is greeted by a man named Pate (*Feast* 45, Samwell V).

114. In the original folktale, Aladdin married a woman named "Badroulbadour." Badroulbadour is so much more fun to say than Jasmine. Say it with us: *Badroulbadour.*

115. Could this answer our question about Jaqen's association with the god of fire?

prayers. And without a doubt, she ain't never had a friend like him.

FAN THEORY FUN:
IS SYRIO A FACELESS MAN?

SYRIO FOREL IS the Prince Rogers Nelson of *Game*: tiny, but potent. Despite Syrio's seemingly diminutive role in the story, devoted fans insist the famously talented dancing master is far more important than his greatest hits. If it's been a while since you last read the first novel or viewed the first season, here is a one-sentence refresher course:

Knowing that his youngest daughter is unhappy with the social expectations of her gender assignment, Ned employs a famous "water dancer" named Syrio to teach Arya swordplay before having to defend her from Lannister henchmen and dying off-screen because he had to fight an armed and armored Meryn Trant with a stick.

This summary (albeit grammatically convoluted) will meet the approval of most fans. Aside from Syrio's wonderfully lyrical instructions and the enchanting gaze of (actor) Miltos Yerolemou, this is about the gist of Syrio Forel. Some devotees will vociferously argue that the First Sword of Braavos is still alive and dancing like it's 1999.[116] After all, Syrio's death leaves far too many questions unanswered.

Can we really trust the finality of any off-screen or subtext death? Are we to believe that the laughable Meryn Trant could best the quick and deadly Syrio Forel? How could Martin murder such a beloved character with such expressive eyeballs?[117] Unsatisfied by the usual answers

116. See for example, see the post by "Mcknuckles" on A Forum of Ice and Fire, May 23, 2011. The post is titled "Syrio Forel = Jaqen H'ghar?" It is by no means the first post on this topic but it captures most of the arguments for and against. Also "Mcknuckles" is an excellent *nom de plume*.

117. Ahem. Well, let's just move on. We got the feels there for a moment.

to these questions, a subset of the GoT-hivemind began asking the ultimate question: *what if Jaqen H'ghar is the artist formerly known as Syrio?*

Both Syrio and Jaqen have connections to Braavos, both men are skilled killers, and both are focused on Arya's development and overall well-being.[118] Moreover, consider how easy it is to connect the dots between the exit of Syrio and the arrival of Jaqen.

- We last see Syrio in King's Landing—*what if he was captured instead of killed?*
- When we meet Jaqen soon afterward, he claims to have been in the black cells of King's Landing.

We know in retrospect that Jaqen can change his appearance at will. Perhaps he was in the guise of Syrio (or *vice versa*) and simply took the life and visage of a fellow prisoner in the black cells?[119] In their first meeting, Jaqen tells Arya: "A man does not choose his companions in the black cells." From Arya's perspective, Jaqen is "the handsome one with the red-and-white hair... Something about the way he talked reminded her of Syrio; it was the same, yet different too" (*Clash* 5, Arya II).

Clearly Martin wants us to associate Jaqen with Syrio, even if only vaguely. Of course, it could be that (from Arya's view) the two simply talk with the same inflection. But remember: Jaqen is seemingly from Lorath; whereas Syrio is from Braavos. We shouldn't assume that they have the same accents. Yet the two men are *the same, yet different too*. Arya seems to sense a similarity in their voices that is difficult to describe. Arya is intelligent and perceptive, and Syrio has taught her his most valuable lesson on being a warrior: "seeing, the true seeing, that is the heart of it." Perhaps that would indicate that her observations and intuitions should

Fan Theory Fun:
Is Syrio a Faceless Man?

118. Syrio's famous line about saying "Not today!" to the God of Death is a show-only quote. His association with the theology of the Faceless Men seems absent (or subtext) in Martin's original story.

119. Detractors point out that the three prisoners in Yoren's paddywagon seem to have been in the black cells while Ned was still Hand of the King (i.e. concurrent with the apparent freedom of Syrio Forel). If Jaqen was in jail at this early stage, it makes it less likely that he and Syrio are the same person. Supporters of the theory maintain that Jaqen is capable of super-ninja trickeration. We find this argument persuasive enough to keep the case file open. Like Mulder, we *want* to believe.

be given more weight than your average 11 year-old wannabe assassin.

And that, wise reader, is the best argument we can muster for the Syrio = Jaqen fan theory. There are perhaps more hints to mine but they require reading between lines, building upon inferences, and the wishful thinking of sweet summer children. The heart wants what the heart wants.

When asked directly if Syrio died at the hands of Meryn Trant, Martin pointed to the near impossibility of Syrio's predicament. Then he advised the asker to "draw your own conclusions."[120]

120. So Spake Martin Archive, Nov. 15, 2005.

Aha! A smoking gun . . . that Martin doesn't like to be asked such questions. Or maybe it means that Syrio is dead and it should be obvious.[121] Or maybe it means that Martin hasn't decided what to do with the plot so that Syrio is both alive and dead *à la* Schrödinger's cat. Whatever the case, Martin's response wasn't a definitive rejection.

121. Or maybe it means that it should be obvious that Syrio is dead because, if it isn't obvious, it would ruin the big reveal that Syrio and Jaqen are really the Night's King who is really a secret Targaryen who is really Bakkalon of the Steel Angels.

Does this mean that there is a slim possibility that Syrio/Jaqen is skipping back and forth from Braavos to Oldtown? *Just so.*

BIRD'S-EYE VIEW: ALL MEN MUST DIE

*V*ALAR MORGHULIS IS the phrase most associated with the Faceless Men. From Martin's pen, it only shows up in Arya's point-of-view chapters. It means "all men must die" and it recalls the perilous conditions of the first Faceless Man in the volcanic mines of the Valyrian Freehold. While thousands of slaves were praying to hundreds of gods, each had this in common: they would all eventually bow before death.

In the HBO adaptation, however, *valar morghu-lis* is a larger world-building detail. Arya repeats it several times but it also features in the dialogue of Dany (S03E03, "Walk of Punishment"), Melisandre (S03E06, "The Climb"), and Daario (S03E08, "Second Sons"). We wonder if the second life of this phrase might tell us something about the larger political agenda of the show. Specifically, we wonder if the showrunners might be telling us that all *males* must die—or, at least, the men vying for the Iron Throne.

Let's start with the War of Five Kings. After the death of Robert Baratheon, the five royal claimants were Joffrey Baratheon, Stannis Baratheon, Renly Baratheon, Balon Greyjoy, and Robb Stark. In the HBO series, all five of these would-be kings are dead (not like *The Search for Spock* dead, or *Batman vs. Superman* dead, but *really* dead). Moreover, each death has cleared the way for a powerful woman. Let's take each in turn:

1. **Joffrey Baratheon** – his death makes way for Margaery's empowerment and Cersei's coronation (show only)

2. **Stannis Baratheon** – his death quashes his rebellion but Melisandre continues to impact the politics of Westeros (show only)

3. **Renly Baratheon** – after his death, both Margaery and Brienne latch onto a house with more political power; both women seem far more important to the overall plot

4. **Balon Greyjoy** – his death did not make Asha/Yara queen but Dany's conquest may improve her claim; again, her impact on the story is far more significant in comparison

5. **Robb Stark** – his death quashes his rebellion but eventually Sansa becomes Lady of Winter-

fell (show only); the rise of Lady Stoneheart also becomes possible (book only)

These five kings learn the hard way that all men must die, many before their time. In contrast, the one would-be queen of Westeros continues to ascend.

At the end of season seven, the key political forces in Westeros include Dany at Dragonstone, Cersei in King's Landing, and Sansa and Arya in Winterfell. At first glance, Jon (secret-Targ) Snow is the exception to the rule. He is, after all, decidedly male and might have the strongest claim the Iron Throne once his true identity is known. But remember the rule: *valar morghulis*; all men must die. Jon may be King in da Norf! but he's also been stabbed to death.

The clearest evidence for the gender-specific meaning of the phrase is Dany's joke (S03E03, "Walk of Punishment"). Dany explains to Missandei that serving her will be dangerous. Missandei replies, valar morghulis. Dany translates, "Yes, all men must die." Then she adds, "But we are not men."

We're not overly invested in building an outcome from a single joke. Admittedly, this is a weak argument. We don't think that every male character will be put down so that Dany or her dead(ish) boyfriend can rule. But it is highly likely that the men who don't die will end up serving in Dany's remade kingdom. *Valar dohaeris.*

Only the Trees Remember

THE WEIRDIFICATION OF BRAN STARK

13

The living know that they will die, but the dead know nothing; they have no more reward, and even the memory of them is lost.

—QOHELET

Types of Reanimation
- right wights, wrong wights, and human wights
- skin-changing second life
- literary tomfoolery
- phoenix typology (via fireproof hotties)

Characters who Ought to be Dead
- Gregor Clegane
- Coldhands
- Beric Dondarrion
- Brynden Rivers
- Varamyr Sixskins
- Jon Snow
- Catelyn Stark
- Daenerys Targaryen

Characters who Enact Literary Resurrection
- Sandor Clegane
- Tyrion Lannister
- Mance Rayder
- Bran and Rickon Stark

J UST SOUTHWEST OF the Antler River is one of the North's best-kept banqueting secrets. Locals call it the "cave of the three-eyed crow," or just CTEC. It's one of most exclusive foodie-underground locations in the Haunted Forest. If you're lucky enough to get in, you'll see why. CTEC is reservation-only, unmarked, and underground. But the savvy culinary enthusiast will find it worth the extra effort.

Owner Brynden Rivers and Executive Chef Snowylocks have conspired to create the perfect savory experience: a restaurant with old-world charm and cutting-edge eccentricity. The CTEC menu is seasonal. Winter features a wide variety of goat's cheeses and dried fruits. Their barleycorn-stuffed mushrooms are little bombs of buttery delight. If you're lucky enough to dine after their black-river harvest, ask for the no-eye albino fish. This reviewer recommends the no-eye sautéed in goat's butter, with a side of barley-and-crannog haggis and psychotropic weirwood seeds.

Spelunkers and arborists will appreciate the rhizome décor. The waiting staff is not overly chatty and sometimes altogether unseen. If your party finds itself in a looping vortex of timeless liminality, check for your server behind the stalagmites or in the tunnels leading to the sunless abyss. The buried, half-decomposed demigod will make sure that your experience is infinitely memorable. Don't feel the need to rush through your meal! Relax, enjoy, *linger*. Don't be alarmed if after a half a hundred years you happen to look down to find yourself affixed permanently to a deciduous deity.

DEEP DIVE:
LITERARY RESURRECTION

WELL-SCHOOLED MAESTER WILL learn almost everything he needs to know to counsel nobility and care for wealthy households. Maesters are also the historians and scientists of Westeros. In a sense, they are trained to be analytical thinkers, to test the natural world for repeatable results, and to be judicious with the knowledge they've gained.

They are, therefore, the perfect foil for a high-fantasy landscape. Part of what gives *A Game of Thrones* plausibility is the repeated—indeed relentless—skepticism for dragons, magic, snarks, and grumkins.[122] It's almost as if Westerosi citizens are living on the cusp of the modern age like Anne Boleyn and Galileo, with the odd Nostradamus thrown in for flavor. Someone like Luwin, the maester of Winterfell, may live his entire life without ever witnessing the supernatural.[123]

Westeros is a society advised by maesters, not mages. Because Martin's readers are told relentlessly that dragons are gone from the world, it creates an inevitable sense of hope for their return. He is able to pay this off at the end of the book with the resurrection of dragons. It's a remarkable achievement considering the genre. First, every reader anticipated it. Second, dragons are a dime a dozen in fantasy literature. Fantasy authors have wallpapered the place with dragons. But, somehow, Martin tricks us into adopting a maester's worldview just long enough to be thrilled by the resurrection.

122. Yes, we know it's also spelled "grumpkins" with a p. Take it up with George.

123. That said, Qyburn claims to have witnessed a ghost. But this wouldn't make him much different than many modern people (*Storm* 44; Jaime VI).

*Only the Trees
Remember:
The Weirdification of
Bran Stark*

124. "Second life" is a phrase that certain skinchangers use to talk about cheating death. Those with the ability to project their consciousness into an animal can do so at the end of their human lives and then have a second life in beast form. Varamyr Sixskins describes and models this process (*Dance*, "Prologue").

125. *Feast* 6, Arya I. Bakkalon, also known as "The Pale Child," is actually Martin paying homage to himself and his "The Thousand Worlds" science fiction universe. Bakkalon is an inversion of the Christ mythos, created by a traumatized humanity in the far future after being nearly wiped out by an alien threat. Whereas Christ is thought of as the "Prince of Peace," Bakkalon bears a sword. Instead of preaching "blessed are the peacemakers," Bakkalon preaches genocide. Instead of the Good Shepherd who loves and cares for all his sheep, Bakkalon calls his followers wolves. For more, see "And Seven Time Never Kill Man!" George R.R. Martin, 1975.

In it's larger canon, *A Song of Ice and Fire* carries this theme of surprising "second life" to an extreme.[124] Martin's world is built on death. From the Silent Sisters to the followers of Bakkalon,[125] everyone feels the imminence of the GRRM-reaper. Almost everyone assumes the finality of death as the default. In his first point-of-view chapter, Tyrion observes that "death is so terribly final" (*Game* 9, Tyrion I). This sounds about right on first hearing. But after five books and seven seasons of study at Martin's School for the Mostly Dead, we know that Tyrion is wrong.

There are a variety of ways to return from the dead in Martin's world. You can climb onto a funerary pyre. You can transfer your soul into an animal. You can become a reanimated wight—fire or ice, take your pick. There are even varieties of ice-wight revivification. For example, would you rather be like undead "Coldhands" who seems to have some form of rebellious self-awareness? Or would you rather be a mindless, garden-variety ice thrall? (We know this isn't really a debate; Coldhands gets to ride an elk.) *So no, Tyrion, death is not terribly final.* You can get an axe to the face and return a few chapters later. Tyrion was one of the many *literary* resurrections in Martin's world and yet another way to echo the great Syrio Forel: *not today*. In Martin's narrative you can say "not today" even if you died yesterday.

Deep Dive: Literary Resurrection

Literary resurrection, as we see it, is when the story describes an event that looks (either to the reader or those within the story) like a character has died but for some unlikely reason shows up alive later in the story. This, of course, is what happened with Gandalf—a literary experience that bothered a young George Martin (more on this below). Other examples would include Andy Dufresne in *The Shawshank Redemption* and Beatrix Kiddo in *Kill Bill, vol. 2*. Both characters are assumed dead, journey through a symbolic underworld, and overcome it with a metaphorical resurrection. We might consider the death and redemption of Sandor Clegane along these lines too. The Hound, as Arya knew him, is dead (*Storm* 74, Arya XIII). But Sandor has risen in a new religious guise as "the gravedigger" (*Feast* 31, Brienne VI).

Another type of literary resurrection is the wise ghost. This is usually the close relative or friend of a key character who has died and returns as an apparition. Sometimes these freaktacular friends and family

*Only the Trees
Remember:
The Weirdification of
Bran Stark*

126. We've long suspected that the
witch is actually the Ewok shaman,
"Logray."

convey a crucial bit of information. Shakespeare does
this with Hamlet's father who names his own murderer.
In the Bible, King Saul goes to the Witch of Endor[126] to
conjure up the spirit of Samuel. (Samuel is mostly just
annoyed to have been disturbed.) Both Obi Wan and
Yoda get to come back to troll Luke in the *Star Wars*
galaxy. Martin is not usually inclined to traffic in ghosts.
He is more inclined to traffic in zombies, wights, and
phoenix-types. That said, he may well bring Jon Snow
back using his direwolf, "Ghost." Many fans guess that
Jon Snow will warg his consciousness into Ghost for
cold storage until he is resurrected in human form, side-
stepping the nasty memory loss and soul fragmentation
reported by Beric Dondarrion.

The most notable exception is Crypt-Ned. At the
end of *Game,* Crypt-Ned visits both Bran and Rickon in
their dreams. *Do we hear echoes of King Hamlet?* Martin
drops a clue that Ned has spoken to Bran about Jon Snow.
"Father was there, and we talked. He was sad." Bran then
vaguely recalls, "It was something to do with Jon, I think"
(*Game* 66, Bran VII). Bran can't quite remember. Keep
in mind that the wise ghost can sometimes reveal a key
plot point. In retrospect, we can guess what Ned might
have shared about Jon's true identity.

As Martin reveals that Crypt-Ned has visited his
sons, Maester Luwin is the mistaken voice of reason. The
reader knows that Ned has been executed. Bran knows
that he spoke with his father (at least in his dream) in
the crypts of Winterfell. Rickon's dream was so vividly
real to him that he went looking for his father near Ned's
future grave. The wildling Osha—not burdened by Citadel skepticism—is open to the possibility that the boys
have dreamt something significant. But Maester Luwin
is erroneously confident that Eddard Stark is still alive,

albeit imprisoned, in King's Landing. Therefore Ned could not possibly have visited his sons the night before.

Luwin chides the boy. After all, *dreams are only dreams*. Osha interjects that some dreams are more and that the Children of the Forest would say the same. Luwin dismisses this notion. He treats it as a legend of a bygone era and scorns the talk of magic entirely. "The man who trusts in spells is dueling with a glass sword," he instructs. *Hokey religions and ancient weapons are no match for a good blaster at your side, kid.*

Deep Dive:
Literary Resurrection

Shade of Samuel: Best known for is poetry, William Blake (1757–1827) was also a painter. In his depiction of 1 Samuel 28, King Saul encounters the apparition of Samuel, the prophet. The Witch of Endor serves as the conjurer. Blake, for some reason, paints Saul as if he's wearing a full-body unitard, perhaps symbolizing his raw, emotional exposure (or passion for interpretive dance). Courtesy of Wikimedia Commons.

When the raven alights with a message from the capitol, the direwolves howl. Even before Maester Luwin reads the bad news, Rickon starts to cry. Bran asks about the note, to which Osha answers, "You know what it is, boy." They all know that Ned's dead before the message is revealed, even Summer and Shaggydog. They all know except Maester Luwin (*Game* 66, Bran VII).

For all of Martin's preoccupation with death, he's created a world where the line between life and death is blurry. He writes a number of resurrections into his story of various types and impacts. These moments foster emotional impact because they are measured against the stubborn disbelief of characters like Maester Luwin.

HISTORICAL BACKDROP: BRÂN THE BLESSED

IN WELSH, THE name *Brân* means "crow." The word for "raven" has a similar root: *cigfran*. We hear echoes of this when the three-eyed crow promises Bran Stark, "you will fly" (*Dance* 13, Bran II). Later Bran enters the skin of a raven as he learns the art of greenseeing. Moreover, a Welsh/English legend about a king named Brân may give us a few interesting parallels to Martin's world.

Brân the Blessed (a.k.a. *Bendigeid Vran*) is an important figure in British mythology. In one story, King Brân of the Britons finds himself in conflict with King Matholwch of Ireland. It all starts when Matholwch proposes an alliance between their two countries by offering to wed Brân's sister, Branwen. The two kings agree to hold the wedding in tents rather than in a house. "No house could ever contain Bendigeid Vran." Did we mention that Brân was a giant?[127] That night Brân's psychopathic half-brother finds out that their sister has

127. Could this be where Martin got the idea for Bran Stark to occupy Hodor's gigantic body from time to time?

148

been married without his consent. His name is Evnissyen and he might be the most deranged character in all mythology.

> *And behold one day, Evnissyen, the quarrelsome man of whom it is spoken above, came by chance into the place, where the horses of Matholwch were, and asked whose horses they might be. "They are the horses of Matholwch king of Ireland, who is married to Branwen, thy sister; his horses are they."*
>
> *"And is it thus they have done with a maiden such as she, and moreover my sister, bestowing her without my consent? They could have offered no greater insult to me than this," said he. And thereupon he rushed under the horses and cut off their lips at the teeth, and their ears close to their heads, and their tails close to their backs, and wherever he could clutch their eyelids, he cut them to the very bone, and he disfigured the horses and rendered them useless.* [128]

Historical Backdrop: Brân the Blessed

This put a bit of a damper on the wedding reception. King Matholwch leaves in a huff and decides to go back to Ireland without saying goodbye.[129] Brân sends emissaries to Matholwch to try to make things right with him but the Irish king is still pissed. Brân promises to replace the horses. "And beside that, as an atonement for the insult he shall have a staff of silver, as large and as tall as himself, and a plate of gold of the breadth of his face. . . and we will make peace in any way he may desire." This gets Matholwch's attention.

128. All quotations from *Mabinogion* are from the translation by Lady Charlotte Guest, 1877; sacred-texts.com.

129. The French should have never been granted the patent on ghosting. The Irish clearly have prior art. A.k.a. the "Irish Goodbye."

149

Ravens of the Tower of London: These Ravens (Jubilee and Munin) are kept by the ravenmaster at the Tower of London. According to a centuries-long tradition, a group of ravens are kept there to protect the crown. Tradition holds that if the ravens are removed, Britain will crumble (or Brexit itself to death). And while the relative merits of constitutional monarchies can be debated, it is an objective fact that a country employing a tower ravenmaster is Fonzie-level cool. Photography by Colin; courtesy of Wikimedia Commons.

Then Brân sweetens the deal, "I will give unto thee a cauldron, the property of which is, that if one of thy men be slain to-day, and be cast therein, to-morrow he will be as well as ever he was at the best, except that he will not regain his speech." Did we mention that Brân had a resurrection cauldron? No? Well, he got it from an ugly, yellow-haired Irish giant with a wife twice his height. But we digress.

King Matholwch happily returns to Ireland with gifts and his new bride, Branwen. She becomes pregnant and gives birth to a son. All seems to be going well. But a few of the other Irishmen can't let go of the insulting, horse-mutilation episode. So they banish Branwen from the royal bedroom, make her cook for everyone, and tell the local butcher to beat her up daily. Why didn't her husband, *the king*, stop this abuse? The story doesn't say. But Branwen had a plan.

Historical Backdrop: Brân the Blessed

> *Branwen reared a starling in the cover of the kneading trough, and she taught it to speak, and she taught the bird what manner of man her brother was. And she wrote a letter of her woes, and the despite with which she was treated, and she bound the letter to the root of the bird's wing, and sent it towards Britain.*

Brân gets the message and decides that Matholwch and his men need a royal beat down. Brân the Blessed "caused sevenscore and four countries" to go to war with him against Ireland. After some treating followed by some tricking, Evnissyen the psychopath reenters the story. The British and Irish are about to make peace when Evnissyen meets his nephew (son of Branwen and Matholwch) for the first time. "Wherefore," said Evnissyen, "comes not my nephew the son of my sister unto me? Though he were not king of Ireland, yet willingly would I fondle the boy." We're pretty sure that *fondle* means something different in this context, but we *did* say Evnissyen is deranged. So the crazy uncle has Branwen's boy on his knee when he decides to burn him alive.

130. This sounds like a Gregor
Clegane move.

*Only the Trees
Remember:
The Weirdification of
Bran Stark*

131. In Westerosi legend, there is an
eight-foot knight named Ser Clarence Crabb. He collected the heads
of knights, pirates, lords, wizards,
and a king. His wife has the magical
ability to bring the heads back to life.
The heads speak to Clarence, giving
him advice, and they whisper to each
other (*Feast*, 14, Brienne III). From a
comparative religions point of view,
this is interesting because the soul
was thought to reside in the head in
Celtic thought.

"Then he arose and took up the boy by the feet, and
before any one in the house could seize hold of him, he
thrust the boy headlong into the blazing fire."[130]

The burning child, it seems, causes a stir and the
battle resumes. After a day and night of battle, Evnissyen
realizes that the Irishmen are simply resurrecting their
dead soldiers with the magic cauldron. Evnissyen is a
psycho, but he's pretty crafty. He hides among the dead
Irish soldiers. The next day he is thrown in the cauldron.
Once inside, he is able to destroy the cauldron but kills
himself in the process.

In the end, only eight Britons escaped back to
London (Branwen among them). Brân the Blessed,
however, was hit with a poison dart in the foot. Brân is
near death when he commands his comrades to cut off
his own head. The defeated Britons carry Brân's giant,
severed head back to London. Along the way, the head
continues to speak so that it can entertain them and keep
them in good spirits.[131] As they traveled, "there came
three birds, and began singing unto them a certain song,
and all the songs they had ever heard were unpleasant
compared thereto."

Eventually, Brân's head is buried upon his request
in London on the White Mount (under the eventual
Tower of London) with his head facing France. According to legend, the head would protect Britain from
invasion. Some believe—although it is disputed—that
the captive ravens that continue to occupy the Tower
of London are connected in some way to the legend of
Brân the Blessed.

CHARACTER STUDY: BRAN

BRANDON STARK JOURNEYS from cute to creepy with a few pit stops in Annoyingville. Worse, in the television adaptation, he is forced to undergo *puberty*. By the time Sam reunites with him in Winterfell, Bran has evolved to something either more or less than human. "I became the Three-Eyed Raven." Sam has become something of an expert on the history and legends of the North. But Sam is at a loss, "Oh . . . I don't know what that means." Bran's answer is that he can see events happening all over the place—past and present. He's becoming more like a Heart Tree or a time-traveling stalker (show only; S07E07, "The Dragon and the Wolf").

It's common for there-and-back-again heroes to experience some kind of re-entry alienation. In Bran's case, he has transformed—becoming godlike—since Sam first met him at the Nightfort. His emotional distance from Sansa, who last knew him as a wall-climbing 7-year-old, is even more dramatic. Judging from what he becomes in season seven, Bran is almost the perfect embodiment of the Hero's Journey.

Bran is beckoned to the North and given aid from a magical bird. He passes the threshold of the Wall with the help of Sam, is helped repeatedly by Meera and Jojen, and is mentored by Bryden Rivers. He literally descends into a hole to transform himself into someone (or something) more enlightened. He is able to see his father again (albeit in a limited way) and undergoes an ego-shattering evolution. Finally, Bran returns to his former home (show only) with his newly acquired gifts from the gods.[132]

Bran is emotionally distant from Sansa and Meera because he has a transformed sense of self. He tells

132. Compare also Richard Preston, "The Hero's Journey in Game of Thrones: Brandon Stark," Winter is Coming; winteriscoming.net, 2016.

Meera, "I remember what it felt like to be Brandon Stark. But I remember so much else now" (S07E04, "The Spoils of War"). He tells Sam, "I remember everything" (S07E07, "The Dragon and the Wolf"). Both of these are show-only details but they extend an important book theme: memory.

The Hero's Journey: Popularized by Joseph Campbell (1904–1987), the hero's journey is a pattern that charts a hero's adventure, challenges, awakening, and return. Courtesy of Wikimedia Commons.

As he's undergoing his most intense transformation, Lord Brynden (now more tree than man) tells Bran that men are forgetful. "Only the trees remember," Brynden says cryptically. Bran asks what this means and Jojen explains, "The secrets of the old gods." Later on, Leaf tells him, "The trees will teach you. The trees remember" (*Dance* 34, Bran III).

Memory creates identity. It follows, then, that Bran's identity will change as his memories expand. Bran taps into the memories of the old gods and so his core identity must transform. If he does indeed complete his journey, Bran is positioned to become one of the most powerful players on Martin's chessboard. Even if he is just a broken-footed talking head buried below Winterfell (*à la* Brân the Blessed), his ability to see far and wide will give the Starks a giant advantage.

FAN-THEORY FUN:
BRAN, THE ETERNAL

THERE ARE LITERALLY dozens of theories about Bran Stark's fate and there are variations on these theories branching out *ad infinitum*. Bran is the Night King. Bran is from an alternate universe. Bran is mentoring his younger self through time-travel trickery. Bran caused Aerys Targaryen to go crazy by whispering to him. Bran has been possessed by Brynden Rivers. Bran is the Lord of Light. We have it on good authority that every time a new Bran theory is posted online, HBO defunds a direwolf scene.

With this in mind, we'll showcase a simple theory that was posted on *A Forum of Ice and Fire*. The post asks, "Is Bran god?" The first comment on this post answers, "He's certainly on his way to becoming an old god."[133] We like this answer because it's nuanced, concise, and defensible. Let's take each in turn.

It's nuanced. The initial question seems to assume that there is a singular "god" in *Song*. Or maybe it's just worded awkwardly. So we need to reframe the question a bit: *is Bran a god?* Once reframed, we just need to specify what type of god we're talking about. The "old gods" seem most likely given Bran's geography. Now we need

133. Credit for the question goes to "King17"; credit for the answer goes to "Victarion Chainbreaker," on A Forum of Ice and Fire, January 8, 2017. It is highly probable that other theorists got to this topic first. But we favor succinct answers when it comes to fan theories.

to take inventory of where Bran is in the story. He's not an old god *yet*. It is probable, however, that Bran will eventually merge with a weirwood tree. In fact, Brynden uses the word "wed." As a greenseer, Bran will be married to the weirwood network. This suggests Bran is on his way to some sort of infusion within Heart Tree divinity.

It's concise. Thank you for being concise, VC.

It's defensible. According to Brynden Rivers, the first "singers" (a.k.a. Children of the Forest) carved eyes in weirwood trees to wake them up. This means that the Heart Trees are animated by some kind of life force. (Jedi masters don't lie about *everything*; sometimes they get it right.) Once the faces of the Heart Trees were carved, the greenseers were able to inhabit the trees and look through their eyes. In Bran's training, the first tree he inhabits allows him to see the godswood at Winterfell. Eventually, Bran will have *a thousand eyes* and *a hundred skins*.[134] More importantly, once inside the trees, greenseers "linger long indeed" (*Dance* 34, Bran III).

Eventually greenseers die and then enjoy a second life inside the Heart Trees. Jojen explains, "Maesters will tell you that the weirwoods are sacred to the old gods. The singers believe they *are* the old gods. When singers die they become part of that godhood" (*Dance* 34, Bran III). Assuming that Bran will die (all men must) it makes sense that he will continue on as part of the godhood.

We will end this section with a question of our own: are the old gods simply the ancient souls of second-life greenseers? It's possible. It could be that, back in Dawn of Days, weirwood trees were animated by life in the same way animals were. But once a greenseer died she or he entered the Heart Trees for a second life (a weirwood lives forever if left undisturbed). The result would be a mix of animism and ancestral worship by later generations.

134. In some ancient cultures one of the key distinctions between humans and gods were that humans could only occupy one body, whereas gods could occupy many. In ancient Assyrian thought, for example, a god like Adad (a weather god) could be labeled by the region of worship. In some ancient contracts, "Adad of Kurba-il" is listed alongside "Adad of Alep" as if the two gods were distinct. But from an Assyrian perspective, there was a sense in which these were the same god occupying different bodies. Thus there was fluidity between fragmentation and wholeness in divinity. For more see, Benjamin D. Sommer, *The Bodies of God and the World of Ancient Israel* (New York: Cambridge University Press, 2009).

Dante and Virgil in the Wood: Engraving by Gustave Doré
(1861) of Dante's Inferno, Canto XIII. As Dante and Virgil
enter the wood of self-murders, they see that several human
souls now occupy trees.

BIRD'S-EYE VIEW:
LIFE, DEATH, AND NEW LIFE

THIS CHAPTER BEGAN by listing several characters who ought to be dead by maester logic.
By Citadel commonsense, Catelyn should have
continued to decompose in the river. Dany should have
died on a funerary pyre. Varamyr should not be able to

project his soul for a bestial second life. Gregor should have met his end on the business end of a poisoned blade. The list goes on.

We've also established that Martin likes to play with literary resurrection. Dany's miraculous emergence from the fire is phoenix symbolism. The backstory of Aeron Damphair's drowning is a literary allusion to baptism (*Feast* 1, Aeron 1). Bran and Rickon are clearly dead—murdered by Theon—from Catelyn's point of view. The list goes on.

Bird's-eye View:
Life, Death, and New Life

Twelfth-Century Phoenix Detail: This is a pictorial detail from the Aberdeen Bestiary. Courtesy of Wikimedia Commons.

Unexpected new life is one of the central literary themes of *A Song of Ice and Fire*. According to Martin, the curious case of Beric Dondarrion is a window into Jon Snow's fate and the larger themes of the book.

Only the Trees Remember: The Weirdification of Bran Stark

Poor Beric Dondarrion, who was set up as the foreshadowing of [Jon's storyline], every time he's a little less Beric," Martin said. "His memories are fading, he's got all these scars, he's becoming more and more physically hideous, because he's not a living human being anymore. His heart isn't beating, his blood isn't flowing in his veins, he's a wight, but a wight animated by fire instead of by ice, now we're getting back to the whole fire and ice thing.[135]

135. Rebecca Hawkes, "George R. R. Martin: 'Gandalf felt like a cheat - coming back from the dead change characters,'" telegraph.co.uk; July 14, 2017.

Clearly, Beric, Jon, and Lady Stoneheart are not phoenix-types. These aren't cocoon-to-butterfly events. There is something fundamentally unnatural about these resurrections.[136]

136. Memory again is key. As Beric's memory continues to deteriorate, so too does his identity. We wonder if Jon will experience something similar in *Winds* or *Dream*. Contrast this with Bran who transforms because his memory (i.e. identity) has expanded dramatically beyond his personal memories.

So while it's true that resurrection is a key theme, Martin has made a conscious decision to part ways with Tolkien.

The Red Wedding for me in Lord of the Rings is the mines of Moria, and when Gandalf falls—it's a devastating moment! I didn't see it coming at 13 years old, it just totally took me by surprise. Gandalf can't die!

And then in the next book, he shows up again, and it was six months between the American publications of those books, which seemed like a million years to me. So all that time I thought Gandalf was dead, and now he's back and now he's Gandalf the White. And, ehh, he's more or less the same as always, except he's more power-ful. It always felt a little bit like a cheat to me. And as I got older and considered it more, it also seemed to me that death doesn't make you more powerful.

Bird's-eye View: Life, Death, and New Life

This theme, then, is borrowed from Tolkien just as Tolkien borrowed it from Catholic doctrine. But Martin—in typical Martin fashion—has subverted it. The unexpected new life we encounter in *Song* still carries the stink of death. It is also a reminder that the natural cycles of life are off-kilter in Westeros. Many of Martin's characters follow the natural cycles of life, but many don't. At the macro-level, the entire cycle of seasons of the planetos is off-kilter.

In this world, winter can last for decades or more because the seasons are tied to magic. Winter brings death. Put another way, death dominates when ice magic runs amok. Conversely, dragon magic (includ-ing the increase of "fire wights") brings unexpected new life with it.

The essential battle in Martin's story is between larger elemental forces. Recently Martin has confirmed what fans long suspected. The real enemy in Westeros is climate change:

The people in Westeros are fight-ing their individual battles over power and status and wealth. And those are so distracting them that they're ignoring

Only the Trees Remember: The Weirdification of Bran Stark

the threat of "winter is coming," which has the potential to destroy all of them and to destroy their world. And there is a great parallel there to, I think, what I see this planet doing here, where we're fighting our own battles. We're fighting over issues, important issues, mind you — foreign policy, domestic policy, civil rights, social responsibility, social justice. All of these things are important. But while we're tearing ourselves apart over this and expending so much energy, there exists this threat of climate change, which, to my mind, is conclusively proved by most of the data and 99.9 percent of the scientific community. And it really has the potential to destroy our world. And we're ignoring that while we worry about the next election . . . All of these things are important issues. But none of them are important if, like, we're dead and our cities are under the ocean.[137]

137. Matt Miller, "George R.R. Martin Explains the Real Political Message of Game of Thrones," esquire.com; Oct 17, 2018.

In the end, *A Song of Ice and Fire* is a story of life and death and new life. The projected title of the final book is telling: *A Dream of Spring*. We guess, therefore, that some sort of macro-ecological resurrection (e.g. the return of dragons) will make *Spring* possible. But most of the players on this stage do not have a wide enough or long enough view of the world to see the big picture. Even the maesters lack the necessary institutional memory to know that death is at the door. And most of the politicians invested in dragon magic cannot see far enough into the future to know its true value.

We can hope that Tyrion is able to think a few extra chess moves ahead. We can hope that Bran is able to see far enough and wide enough to understand the macro game. But, as Bloodraven says, "Men forget. Only the trees remember" (*Dance* 34, Bran III).

Bird's-eye View:
Life, Death, and New Life

Gods be Good?

A CLOSING REFLECTION

THE PEOPLE OF Westeros have an idiom. "Gods be good," they say, or "gods be kind." It remains to be seen whether this is even possible. There are indeed gods in the Martin multiverse, but they don't seem inclined to goodness or kindness.

Brienne, who is as pious as any knight you'll meet, senses the truth of it. She privately confesses, "The gods don't care about men, no more than kings care about peasants" (*Clash* 22, Catelyn II). Brienne continues to pray to the Seven before she sleeps and continues to act on the authority of kings, lords, and ladies. Deep down, however, she believes that the only good king (Renly) was murdered. So she has good reason to doubt the sympathy of gods. Maybe they are hopelessly detached from the interests of the realm (book only).

What Brienne quietly doubts, Tyrion openly mocks. Tyrion's trial has gone sideways (according to the plans of Tywin) and he has demanded a trial by combat. This tradition is a way to find justice by letting the gods decide. As he waits for the combat to begin—the blood sport that will judge whether he is guilty of regicide—he waxes theological with Jaime. "Trial by combat: deciding a man's guilt or innocence in the eyes of the gods by having two other men hack each other to pieces." Then our favorite lion cub winks knowingly at his big brother, "Tells you something about the gods" (S04E08, "The Mountain and the Viper"; show only).

The gallows humor of Jaime and Tyrion then turns to "Cousin Orson." The brothers recall him from their childhood. Orson was preoccupied with killing beetles. They call him "simple" but Tyrion found him fascinating. In this scene, Orson was something like a god who towered above the beetles and imposed his singular will upon them.

Tyrion recalls his complete inability to decipher his cousin's purpose. When he asked Orson to explain, he only to said "smash them!" like some medieval Hulk. "I was the smartest person I knew," Tyrion remembers, "Certainly I had the wherewithal to unravel the mysteries that lay at the heart of a moron."[138] At the end of the day, Orson's higher-life-form intentions remain a mystery.

As the scene ends, the bells toll from the Great Sept. The bells remind us of the previous conversation about trial by combat and the gods.[139] If the most intelligent guy in our story cannot decipher the thoughts of Cousin Orson, how can anyone hope to explain the mind of the gods?

There is, of course, a darker interpretation of this scene. *What if the gods are like Orson? And what if warriors like Gregor and Oberyn are simply beetles by comparison?* If so, this means that the gods of thrones have no great plans for good or ill. If they exist, they are simply impersonal cosmic forces devoid of sympathy or empathy. The gods, in this view, have more in common with volcanoes and avalanches than they have with someone like Tyrion.

This may well be the best explanation for the Seven, R'hllor, the Great Shepherd, and maybe even the White Walkers. It could be that negotiating with the Others is as futile as negotiating with a snowstorm.

But what of the imminent gods in the story? These are the gods who happen to have point-of-view chapters: Brandon Stark and Daenerys Targaryen. Bran and Dany,

138. Again, this extends a show-only conversation. There is no Lannister cousin matching this description in Martin's original telling. There is a mention to "drooling cousins" (*Dance* 27, Tyrion VII) and there is a character named Ser Orson Stone (*Dance* 25, The Windblown). But "Cousin Orson" is an invention of the showrunners. It is also worth noting that Jaime and Tyrion both acknowledge that speaking this way of Orson is an act of cruelty. Even so, modern students of disability studies will caution us against reductionist views of "the afflicted" (Jaime's words).

139. Credit is due to "Ann from California" who provided a like-minded interpretation on the listener feedback portion of *Game of Thrones: The Podcast*; "408 – The Mountain and the Viper," June 3, 2014. Ann pointed out that the "gong, gong, gong" of the bells mirrors the "kun, kun, kun" of Orson's smashing (1:07:30).

no doubt, are sentient. These players are much more than unthinking magical forces, although they have become conduits for such forces. It isn't hard to imagine royal pretenders like Stannis or Euron also harnessing this kind of power. Here we have a supposed covenant between a supernatural force and a human mediator. If so, we are reminded of the wry wisdom of Mushroom, "The gods chose our new regents ... and it would seem that the gods are just as thick as lords" (*Fire and Blood*, "The Lysene Spring and the End of Regency").

A Closing Reflection

If the weirdification of Bran Stark is any indication, becoming godlike also means becoming less relatable, less personal, and less focused on the particular struggles of individuals. As Bran's memories and concerns reach far and wide, his own family ties are less crucial to his new identity. Martin seems to be playing with the consequences of omniscience (being all-knowing) or, at least, Bran is inching closer to expansive knowledge surpassing his own mortal coil.

On the other hand, Dany has become godlike (in the Greco-Roman sense) by way of superhuman power. Rather than diminishing her ego and interests in her immediate relationships, Dany's force of personality emerges like a phoenix. Here Martin seems to be playing with the consequences of power. The questions of Tyrion and Varys remain crucial: is she inching closer to becoming a mad queen?

No doubt, Dany and Bran are protagonists. If Martin's promise of a "bittersweet" ending comes to fruition, one (if not both) of these characters will triumph over the White Walkers. There is no promise, however, for Dany's accumulation of power to enhance her essential goodness. Bran's kindness has not been helped by his ascent to godhood.

In the end, no one is purely kind or good in *A Song of Ice and Fire*. More to the point, we should expect even less virtue from an icy tree spirit or a fiery apex predator. The best hope for the Seven Kingdoms is that at least a few of our favorite characters will remember what made them human before they ascended to divinity.

This brings us to the matter of redemption. Last we left Bran, he was becoming something less human. Arya certainly has us worried too. The question of the redemption of our favorite characters is open to debate. It's still unclear if Martin even knows which characters are closer to redemption and which are not. We do know that the question interests him. In his own words, Martin finds "the question of redemption fascinating." He continues,

> *I'm not religious now but I was raised a Catholic. . . the Catholic Church teaches that you go to confession and you are forgiven for your sins. Even terrible sins! But certainly our society doesn't necessarily deal with that; we don't forgive people. Even I don't forgive people. I recognize. I'm a grey character myself here.*[140]

140. "An Evening with George R. R. Martin and Publisher Tom Doherty at the Brown University Library," youtube.com, Oct. 30, 2014.

The complex problems of redemption are still unfolding in this story. As readers and viewers we feel differently about Jaime and Sandor than we once did. These are morally grey characters by design and yet they seem to be on redemptive journeys. If a Hound can reach out into the darkness and find his humanity, perhaps a tree spirit, a wolf girl, and a dragon queen can too.

GLOSSARY OF SNARKS
AND GRUMKINS

ALCHEMISTS | A guild claiming to be studied in ancient wisdom, including supernatural know-how. By the time of the Baratheon period, their practical abilities are mostly impotent. The exception to their flaccidity is an ability to produce wildfire. Wildfire is a highly flammable and explosive substance, sometimes used in warfare.

AUROCHS | A large ox-like beast of burden once numerous (now rare) in Westeros.

AZOR AHAI | A legendary warrior who lived thousands of years before the Baratheon period. He wielded a sword named Lightbringer that was forged by plunging the blade into the heart of his wife, Nissa Nissa (a.k.a. murder). Despite his homicidal legacy, followers of R'hllor hope for his return. Depending on the tradition, he is variously named Eldric Shadowchaser, Hyrkoon the Hero, Neferion, and Yin Tar.

BAKKALON | A god venerated in Essos associated with war and death. He is one of the gods appropriated by the Faceless Men. Statues of Bakkalon (also called the Pale Child) depict him as a young, pale boy with a sword.

BALERION THE BLACK DREAD | *See* DRAGONS.

BASILISKS | Large, venomous beasts native to the jungles of Yi Ti. They are sometimes used for entertainment in fighting pits. Their venom and blood are highly poisonous and can be used to enhance blades. They vary is size, but some reports measure them twice the size of lions.

BEARDED PRIESTS OF NORVOS | Theocratic leaders of Norvos and the mediators of a purity religion. Their god's name is neither spoken nor written and is unknown to outsiders. They are warriors of renown, preferring long axes. They teach that sex is only for the purpose of procreation and should not be practiced for the sake of pleasure. In short, they are killjoy killers. Also, they have beards.

BEASTLINGS | *See* SKINCHANGERS.

BLACK GOAT | An ungulate worshipped in Qohor. Followers sacrifice cattle and horses daily in his honor. Human sacrifice is practiced on holy days and in times of great distress. On holy days criminals are offered as a blood sacrifices. In times of national crisis, children with noble blood are sometimes offered. The Black Goat is believed to be a demon by the Bearded Priests of Norvos. Goat eyeballs and pupils are ghastly to behold and probably the source of all evil.

BLACK STONE | Geologic relics from prehistory. Artifacts made of black stone are frequently described as oily (or greasy) and may point to a culture that predates the Children in Westeros. Examples include the Seastone Chair of the Iron Islands, the Toad Stone of the Basilisk Isles, the ruins of Yeen in Sothoryos, and the base of Hightower in Oldtown. *See also* DEEP ONES.

BLIND GOD | *See* BOASH.

BLOODFLIES | Large, purple, bloodsucking insects. These are as disgusting as they sound. Indigenous to Essos, bloodflies lay their eggs in the dead and *dying*. Sweet dreams, summer child!

BLOOD MAGIC | A generic term used of various rituals. The underlying belief is that blood (both of animals and humans) is imbued with power and can be used to garner the favor of gods. Wielding this power can involve drawing blood, dismemberment, or full-body sacrifice. By and large, cultures that do not practice blood magic consider this practice to be dark and dangerous. Those with facility in blood magic are sometimes called bloodmages or maegi.

BLOODMAGES | *See* BLOOD MAGIC.

BOASH | A deity worshipped in Essos, primarily in Lorath, sometimes called the Blind God. Lorathi are typically vegetarians, believe that all life is sacred, and use ego-negating language (e.g. first-person singular pronouns are avoided). Priests of Boash cover their eyes hoping to promote visionary experience.

CENTAURS | Creatures of legend. Some legends of Essos feature these human-horse hybrids that are thought to have existed in prehistory. Others suggest that rumors of centaurs emerged from the fear and confusion of people not familiar with warriors mounted on horseback.

CHILDREN OF THE FOREST | Forest dwellers with special wisdom about the (super) natural world. These so-called "children" or "singers" resided in Westeros before humans. The first human colonizers of Westeros (First Men) judged them to be childlike in size and named them the Children of the Forest. They are the source of the animistic way of life in the North (adopted by the Stark kings and their subjects). Their sages are called greenseers (*see* GREENSEERS). Their worship of nature sometimes includes blood sacrifices to tree deities. *See also* HEART TREES.

CHURCH OF STARRY WISDOM | A minor religion of Essos practiced in certain port cities. The church seems to originate from Yi Ti after the short reign of the Amethyst Empress. Her brother murdered her and called himself the Bloodstone Emperor. According to legend, he practiced dark magic, cannibalism, and rebelled against the traditional Yi Tish gods. In place of tradition, he made the people worship a black stone that fell from the sky (*see* BLACK STONE). Some traditions claim that the Bloodstone Emperor was the first high priest and founder of the church.

CRAB GODS | Little is known of these clerical crustaceans. Some rumors say they are worshipped at Storrold's Point, the site of the wildling settlement Hardhome.

CRAB KING | A lesser deity under the rule of Mother Rhoyne (*see* MOTHER RHOYNE) in Rhoynar mythology. It is said that he, alongside several other deities, sang a song to bring back the sun after a long period of darkness.

DAWN AGE | An era of prehistory before the records of the maesters, also called the Dawn of Days. During this period the "elder races" (presumably the Children and giants) occupied Westeros and practiced nature/ancestral worship. Several mythologies of various cultures trace their beginnings to this era.

DEEP ONES | Creatures of legend. Several myths from various cultures preserve stories about a sea-dwelling people who wreaked havoc on ancient coastal tribes. Some myths suggest that these squishy-fishy villains are hybrid creatures begotten from sea creatures and human women. Some suggest that the Deep Ones represent or serve sea demons. All information about these creatures derives from ancient stories, leading many to doubt their existence. Those who hold to their historical veracity think they once encamped the iron islands and may explain the provenance of black stone. *See also* BLACK STONE.

DIREWOLVES | A rare species of northern wolf. They can grow larger than ponies and can attract large packs of smaller, subservient wolves. Certain skinchangers are able to project their minds into direwolves (*see* WARGS). Otherwise, these great beasts are wild and rare. Their natural enemies include double-crossing Freys and CGI budgets.

DOOM OF VALYRIA | A cataclysmic event that befell Old Valyria when the entire chain of volcanoes (the Fourteen Flames) erupted at once. This obliterated the Valyrian subcontinent, leaving the "Smoking Sea" in its place. It is debated whether it was purely a natural disaster or the result of sorcery gone awry.

DORNISH SAND STEEDS | Horses bred in Dorne but little known elsewhere. Dornishmen boast that these horses can gallop day and night without tiring. They are said to be smaller and weaker than warhorses with longer necks and narrower heads.

DOSH KHALEEN | Widows of deceased Dothraki khals (chieftains). Literally meaning "council of crones" in Dothraki, the Dosh Khaleen is the governing body of Vaes Dothrak. It functions as an arbiter of matters related to ritual and prophecy.

DRAGONBINDER | A six-foot horn said to be made from a dragon horn and Valyrian steel. It is alleged that (when blown properly) the blower will be able to bind dragons (and perhaps other creatures) to his/her will. If blown by a person who has not claimed the horn via blood ritual, the blower will die. The horn is adorned with glowing Valyrian glyphs.

DRAGONS | When mature and free to roam, dragons are the apex predator of Westeros and Essos. They were trained and weaponized by the Valyrians before the Doom of Valyria. The Targaryens (a noble house descending from the Valyrian Freehold) used dragons to conquer Westeros. Dragons can range from house pet-sized to village-sized. The largest of the Targaryen dragons was "Balerion the Black Dread." Balerion's skull grew over the course of two centuries to the size of a carriage. Dragons have the look of great reptiles with bat wings. Sea dragons lack wings but are otherwise no less powerful than their winged counterparts. Dragons are thought to be highly intelligent and are connected in some way with global magic. In *A Song of Ice and Fire*, the return of dragons in Essos enhances the magical abilities of friends and foes alike all over the map. *See also* NAGGA.

DROWNED GOD | The god worshipped on the Iron Islands. Also known as "He who Dwells Beneath the Waves," the Drowned God plucked fire from the sea to create the Ironborn. He then set them to "reaving." Thus the thieving, sacking, and murderous culture of the Ironborn is practiced in homage to this god. He is enthroned beneath the ocean and is constantly warring the Storm God, who resides above the clouds. Priests in service to the Drowned God (Drowned Men) are ritually drowned and resuscitated. They enact this same ritual to new devotees upon initiation.

DROWNED MEN | *See* DROWNED GOD.

DWARF ELEPHANTS | These things are adorable. I mean, just think about how adorable they are. Sadly, they are used as beasts of burden in Volantis because Martin is a sadistic fiend.

ELDER BROTHER | *See* SEPTRIES.

ELDER RACES | *See* DAWN AGE.

FACELESS MEN | A group of assassins with religious gumption. Faceless Men are so named for two reasons. First, seasoned members of their group eschew almost all personal identification, including names, titles, possessions, and self-motivated actions. This is their religious ideal (even if not borne out in praxis). Second, they literally have the power to change their faces. This is a vampiresque "glamouring" ability whereby a person's entire body takes the look and shape of another person. Faceless Men serve the Many-Faced God. In service to this god, the Faceless Men serve as mercy killers. The killing is done to assuage the suffering of those who wish to die. A person may seek death for themselves or a loved one in the House of Black and White. Faceless Men are also contract killers who accept payment on a sliding scale depending on the wealth/resources of the contractee. The House of Black and White functions as temple and monastery for full members and novices. Hundreds of human faces are preserved in their Hall of Faces. Using these faces, the Faceless Men are talented spies and assassins. *See also* MANY-FACED GOD.

FAITH MILITANT | Although disbanded and stripped of power long before the Baratheon period, the Faith of the Seven once employed a branch of religious enforcers. This monkish military takes orders from the High Septon rather than the Iron Throne. The two branches of this military are named the Warrior's Sons and the Poor Fellows.

FATHER OF THE WATERS | | A god of Braavos. The Father of the Waters is venerated on his feast days and at his dedicated temple. According to tradition, he takes a new bride every year. In honor of this festival, his temple is rebuilt annually.

FIREWYRMS | A breed of large reptile. Burrowed in the heart of the volcanic mountains of Old Valyria, these fire-breathers were often encountered by ore-mining slaves. As babies, they are thin as snakes but adults can grow larger than humans. An infestation of juvenile firewyrms might have been responsible for the horrific death of Princess Aerea during the reign of Jaehaerys I.

FISHER QUEENS | A legendary folk. In Sarnor mythology, the Fisher Queens were a wise, beneficent folk who ruled from floating cities. Their domain covered the Silver Sea (great lakes) in northern Essos. The "Tall Men" of Essos trace their lineage to the last king (Huzhor Amai) of this legendary people.

FOUNTAIN OF THE DRUNKEN GOD | A shrine dedicated to a god in Essos. The fountain erected to honor the Drunken God is one of the holy sites of Tyrosh.

FROSTFANGS' GODS | Nameless gods of ill-repute. While most free folk of the True North are thought to worship the old gods, some are rumored to worship "dark gods" that reside underground at the Frostfangs.

GHISCARI GRACES | Holy women of Astapor, Meereen, and Yunkai. These cities of Slaver's Bay trace their lineage to the Ghiscari Empire. As an imperial carryover, each city boasts a "Temple of Graces" inhabited by holy women. Ghiscari religion is polytheistic and promotes ritual combat in homage to the gods. Graces order their rank by color of garb. Red Graces engage in sexually ecstatic ritual. Blue Graces function as healers. Green Graces function as high priestesses. Just as there is only one temple per city, there is only one high priestess per temple. Ghiscari religion claims the sigil of a harpy and feature eagle's talons, a scorpion's tail, and the wings of a bat. Variations on this image are displayed on each city's flag.

GHOST OF HIGH HEART | A "ghost" described variously as an albino with red eyes, a dwarf, and a woods witch. She is rumored to have previously died in the castle fire of Summerhall, yet survives in some form on the sacred hill of High Heart (*see* HIGH HEART). Those who seek her prophecy may hear of her symbolic and prophetic dreams. Her dreams have great affinity with those of greenseers. *See also* GREENSEERS.

GIANT TURTLES | Creatures of religious significance. Venerated as lesser gods by the Rhoynar, these turtles of unusual size are said to be bigger than elephants and reside in the Rhoyne. *See also* MOTHER RHOYNE.

GIANTS | Supersized bipeds. Before the coming of the "First Men" to Westeros, tribes of giants were among the indigenous peoples. They ranged between 10 and 14 feet tall and were allied with the Children of the Forest. In bygone eras, the Jhogwin giants of Essos were twice the size of the northern tribes. In the North, they are covered in hair, like a bear (a bear, a bear!) and speak the language of the First Men. *See also* MACUMBER.

GLASS CANDLES | Magical devices used to see faraway events. It is possible that they are also used to communicate at a distance. They are magical relics from Old Valyria made of obsidian. During the Baratheon period, most believe that these relics are nonfunctional or fraudulent.

GLITTERING GOD | *See* GOD-EMPERORS OF YI TI.

GOD OF DEATH | *See* MANY-FACED GOD.

GOD-EMPERORS OF YI TI | Princes of Yi Ti claiming to be descended from god-emperors. They governed in enormous wealth. For example, Mengo "the Glittering God" Quen ruled from a palace covered (from floors to chamber pots) in gold leaf.

GOD OF TITS AND WINE | *See* TYRION.

GOD-ON-EARTH | An anthropomorphic deity of Yi Ti. According to Yi Ti mythology, he was only son of the Lion of Night and the Maiden-made-of-Light who ruled a vast kingdom in Essos for a millennium. He travelled from region to region with a hundred wives (queens) before ascending to heaven. It is possible, however, that this was just some dude with a high opinion of himself.

GOD'S EYE | *See* ISLE OF FACES.

GODSWIVES | *See* GREAT SHEPHERD.

GREAT LIONS | Big (indeed the biggest) cats. The great lions once roamed the "western hills," although this geography remains vague. They are extinct by the Baratheon period and are remembered only by the Children.

GREAT OTHER | *See* R'HLLOR.

GREAT SEPT OF BAELOR | *See* SEPTS.

GREAT SHEPHERD | A god of Essos. The Great Shepherd is worshipped by the monotheistic folk of Lhazar. This deity is believed to be the shepherd of all tribes and will reward or punish all people according to their deeds. Priestesses in service to the Great Shepherd also function as nurses, midwives, and healers. They are called "godswives."

GREAT STALLION | A sky god of Essos. Very much like the Italian Stallion, the Great Stallion is worshipped by working-class folk and venerated for kicking ass. Unlike Rocky, however, the deity of Vaes Dothrak is associated with equestrian culture. The Great Stallion is believed to ride in the "Night Lands," a mythology stemming from stargazing. The Dothraki believe that their ancestors ride alongside the Great Stallion in the sky. In death, Dothraki who hope to join their ancestors are burned on a pyre so that their souls may rise to the Night Lands.

GREEN MEN | A sacred order isolated on the Isle of Faces. The Green Men are devoted to the care of the weirwood trees on the island. *See also* ISLE OF FACES.

GREENSEERS | Sages associated with northern animism. Their powers include visions of events over great distances, past, present, and perhaps future. Blood sacrifice (sometimes human) is occasionally employed to enhance their power over nature. It is possible that ancient greenseers commanded the waters of sea to destroy a continental land bridge. *See also* HAMMER OF THE WATERS.

GREY KING | The mythological patriarch of the Iron Islands. He is credited with building the first longship and slaying Nagga, the sea dragon. *See also* NAGGA AND YGG.

GRIFFINS | Legendary hybrid beasts. Although none have seen a living griffin, this half-lion/half-eagle creature is depicted on shields, banners, and statues throughout Westeros and Essos. Some rumors suggest that these beasts were worshipped beyond Asshai, in the Shadow Lands.

GRUMKINS | Creatures of superstition. Grumkins (variant: "Grumpkins") are small, dangerous boogeymen featured in stories meant to frighten children. *See also* SNARKS.

HALL OF FACES | *See* FACELESS MEN.

HAMMER OF THE WATERS | A legendary (super)natural weapon of great power. During the war between the "First Men" and elder races, the magic-wielding greenseers destroyed the land bridge between Dorne and Essos. The greenseers sunk the land bridge to slow the colonization of the First Men. Those who hold to this legend claim that hundreds of human sacrifices were required to summon the dark magic. Skeptics argue that the land bridge sunk by way of natural causes. Later, the Children would try this gambit once more, leading to the formation of the swampy "Neck" that separates the North from the other kingdoms of Westeros.

HARPIES | Sexually transmuted deities. *See also* GHISCARI GRACES.

HEART TREES | Gods of the North, also called the "old gods." The countless gods of the Children animated streams, rocks, plants, and trees. Weirwood trees were especially sacred. The Children provided eyes for their gods by carving faces into weirwood trees. These were called Heart Trees and are still prayed to by many folk in the North. It was said that the greenseers (*see* GREENSEERS) could see through the eyes of the Heart Trees. Fearing this ability to spy, southern men cut down all such trees in their region. Heart Trees were often the sites of blood sacrifices (including human sacrifice).

HELLHORN | *See* DRAGONBINDER.

HIGH HEART | A place sacred to worshippers of the old gods. The hill named High Heart in the riverlands was once crowned by 31 weirwood trees. These sacred trees were clearcut by the invading Andals who practiced the Faith of the Seven and targeted the strange tree gods for destruction. Although defended by the First Men and Children, the hill was lost to the Andals and only stumps remain. Many in the riverlands consider this hill to be haunted. *See also* GHOST OF HIGH HEART.

HIGH SEPTON | *See* SEVEN-FACED GOD.

HOODED WAYFARER | A god of Essos. The Faceless Men keep a statue of this deity in the House of Black and White. The impoverished worshippers in Braavos tend to prefer the statue of the Wayfarer. Little more is known of this god from a Westrosi perspective.

HORN OF JORAMUN | A legendary weapon. In the legends of the True North, a king beyond the Wall named Joramun blew a great horn to bring forth giants from the earth. Also called the Horn of Winter, it is believed to have the power to bring down the Wall. *See also* WALL.

HORN OF WINTER | *See* HORN OF JORAMUN.

HOUSE OF BLACK AND WHITE | The singular temple and headquarters of those who serve the Many-Faced God. Located on an island of Braavos, this temple features altars and statues of numerous gods of various faiths. The temple serves as a location for euthanasia as well as a place of worship. The Faceless Men prepare bodies for the creation of magical masks below the temple. Prayer services are held in the temple twice a day. *See also* FACELESS MEN.

HOUSE OF THE UNDYING | *See* WARLOCKS OF QARTH.

HYRKOON THE HERO | A legendary figure. The ancestors of Bayasabhad, Kayakayanaya, and Shamyriana claim that they are the descendants of Hyrkoon the Hero. This is their name for Azor Ahai. *See also* AZOR AHAI.

ISLE OF FACES | A place sacred to worshippers of the old gods. Located in the center of the God's Eye (the largest lake in the Seven Kingdoms). After the war between the "First Men" and the Children, the two groups formed a pact on the island. The pact awarded the open lands of Westeros to the Men; the Children retained the forested wilderness. They agreed that the men would no longer destroy weirwoods. The Children carved faces on every tree on the island so that the gods would witness the pact. Thereafter a sacred order of arborists was formed to care for the island. *See also* GREEN MEN.

KRAKENS | Deep-sea creatures large and strong enough to sink ships. Sailors report that they are squid-like in appearance, although most landlubbers doubt their existence.

LEVIATHANS | Sea monsters. What some Westerosi call "whales."

LIGHTBRINGER | *See* AZOR AHAI.

LION OF NIGHT | A mythological figure. He is the father of the legendary God-on-Earth (*see* GOD-ON-EARTH) whom he sired with the Maiden-made-of-Light. He also functions as a god of judgment who brings punishment in times of wickedness. Some claim he commands an army of demons for this purpose.

LITTLE VALYRIAN | A species of lemur indigenous to the Forest of Qohor. They feature silver fur and violet eye coloring, recalling the features of the peoples of Old Valyria.

LIZARD-LIONS | A crocodilian species that lives in the swamps of the Neck. Lizard-lions are as dangerous as they sound and twice as mean.

LONG NIGHT | A legendarily long season of Winter. In Planetos cosmology, the seasons are irregular and unpredictable. Winters and summers can last for years. One such winter lasted for over a generation. Various mythologies tell of this "Long Night." While these stories boast of different heroic figures and deeds that brought back the sun, they all grant the plausibility of this event.

LORD OF HARMONY | A nude deity. Also called the Butterfly God, this god is thought to protect the island of Naath. He is depicted as a naked, laughing giant. Last seen wandering the Haight-Ashbury looking for a live recording of Bubble Puppy.

LORD OF LIGHT | *See* R'HLLOR.

LORD OF THE SEVEN HELLS | A mythological figure. This being the embodiment of evil according to the teachings of the Faith of the Seven. He commands demons and is generally unpleasant.

MACUMBER | The sky is blue in Martin's multiverse because his characters exist within the eye of a blue-eyed giant named Macumber. Prove us wrong. We dare you. #science

MAEGI | A title that is variously translated as "wise" or "sorceress." The term can also be used as a polemic. In general, a maegi's prowess in the spirit realm exploits the magical properties of human or animal blood via ritual.

MAELYS I | A two-headed warrior. Maelys I or "Maelys the Monstrous" was a member of the Blackfyre Rebellion (claimants for the Iron Throne). He is best known for having a second, smaller head protruding from his neck. Also known for his magnificent strength on the battlefield.

MAIDEN-MADE-OF-LIGHT | A Yi Ti goddess. The Maiden is a sun goddess who turned her back on the people of Yi Ti during the reign of the Bloodstone Emperor (*see* CHURCH OF STARRY WISDOM). According to Yi Tish lore, this caused the Long Night. *See also* LONG NIGHT AND LION OF NIGHT.

MAMMOTHS | Pachyderms standing twenty feet tall and covered in fur. Remaining in their snowy northern habitats, they are sometimes used as mounts by giants.

MANTICORES | Beasts with scorpion-like tails thought to roam the islands of the Jade Sea. Their venom is highly poisonous and sometimes used to enhance blades. Manticores are comparable to iocane powder in terms of deadliness but not nearly as useful to Sicilian geniuses.

MANY-FACED GOD | A Braavosi god. The deity worshipped by the Faceless Men is also named "Him of Many Faces," or (show only) the "God of Death." The House of Black and White in Braavos is a holy site dedicated to this god. The site functions as the temple and the headquarters for the Faceless Men. Within the House of Black and White, statues pay homage to the Stranger, a Heart Tree, the Drowned God, R'hllor, and others. These represent gods venerated in other religious systems. But according to followers of the Many-Faced God, each god simply represents a different face of the same, singular deity. The key element that unites these religions is death, which the Many-Faced God gives as a gift to all people to alleviate suffering. *See also* FACELESS MEN AND HOUSE OF BLACK AND WHITE.

MAZES | Ruins of ancient mazes found throughout Essos. Although their purpose in prehistory remains unknown, some speculate that they were connected to temples. This may be corroborated by the fact that one such sect still exists that practices ritual maze walking as a sacred discipline. The Patternmakers teach that properly walking their maze is the only path to wisdom. *See also* PATTERNMAKER.

MERLING | *See* VARYS.

MERLING KING | A legendary figure. The Merling King is a god generally associated with merlings (mermaids and mermen) in legend. Various cultures throughout Essos and Westeros preserve these legends. Noteworthy among them are the settlements bordering the Narrow Sea.

MERMAIDS | Legendary figures and religious myths. Mer-folk (humanlike but with fish tails) are often called "merlings." Mermaids are featured in various legends. In Ironborn religion, those who return to the Sea to be with the Drowned God are tended to by mermaids.

MOON-PALE MAIDEN | A goddess popular with sailors. She is featured as a statue in the House of Black and White (*see* HOUSE OF BLACK AND WHITE).

MOONSINGERS | Legendary prophets of the Faceless Men. Before the Doom of Valyria, a permanent slave class was kept by the Valyrians. These slaves were employed primarily to mine for ore. Eventually the slaves banded together and escaped using the prophetic visions of moonsingers as their guide. The moonsingers guided the slaves to a secret place shrouded by fog where they lived in hiding. Here they founded the Free City of Braavos.

MOST DEVOUT | An elite committee of the Faith of the Seven. Male and female clerics comprise this group, who are tasked with selecting new High Septons.

MOTHER RHOYNE | The river goddess believed to animate the River Rhoyne, the mightiest of all rivers. She is said to have helped the Rhoynar "water-wizards" in two ways. She whispered secrets to the wizards and allowed them to use upswelling waters as a weapon against their enemies. When used to bring toxic water and fog against the people of Valyria, Mother Rhoyne cursed the Valyrians with greyscale. The river was home to gigantic turtles that grew larger than elephants. The Rhonyar called them the "old men of the river" and believed them to be divine.

MOTHERHOUSES | *See* SEPTRIES.

NAGGA | A legendary sea dragon. In Ironborn lore, Nagga was a dragon so large she fed on krakens. The Grey King defeated Nagga and used her bones to build a longhall. Nagga's Hill is considered sacred to the Ironborn and hosts the choosing of a new king.

NIGHT KING | The eldest and highest ranking White Walker (*see* WHITE WALKERS). In one version of his legend, the Children created the Night King to fight the first human colonizers of Westeros.

NIGHT LANDS | *See* GREAT STALLION.

NIGHT'S KING | A legendary figure. The Night's King is a storied Lord Commander of the Night's Watch who established himself as a king at the Wall. According to one account, he wed a supernatural woman from beyond the Wall.

NIGHT'S WATCH | An ancient order of defenders tasked with overseeing the Wall at the northern border of the Seven Kingdoms. They were originally established to defend humankind against the White Walkers. But as the White Walkers passed out of historical memory and into myth, the order devoted itself to fighting the Free Folk beyond the Wall (whom they labeled "wildlings"). The Free Folk returned the hostility by labeling the Night's Watch "crows." The monkish men of the Night's Watch forsake titles, land, marriage, and progeny to join the group. As such, members are drawn primarily from impoverished men, criminals escaping capital punishment, and boys who cannot otherwise advance their social standing. *See also* WALL.

OLD GODS | Worshipped primarily north of the Neck, the so-named "old gods" are the nature spirits associated with weirwood trees and the rituals of greenseers. *See* CHILDREN OF THE FOREST, HEART TREES, GREENSEERS.

OLD MEN OF THE RIVER | *See* MOTHER RHOYNE.

OTHERS | *See* WHITE WALKERS.

PALE SPIDERS | Pale spiders as large as hounds? We're not going to talk about it.

PATTERNMAKER | The object of worship for the Patternmakers. *See also* MAZES.

PRIESTS OF BAYASABHAD | Clerics of Essos. Only one percent of all men in Bayasabhad are allowed to sire children. The other 99% live their adult lives as eunuchs, priests included. It's not the worst idea in the world.

PRINCE THAT WAS PROMISED | *See* AZOR AHAI.

PYROMANCERS | *See* ALCHEMISTS.

R'HLLOR | A god of (primarily) Essos. Also known as the Red God and the Lord of Light, R'hllor is worshiped in many places throughout Essos and Westeros but especially in in the southern Free Cities such as Volantis, Lys, and Myr. This god is primarily associated with fire and stands against a counterpart deity known as the Great Other. Red Priests and Red Priestesses practice worship variously. Some incorporate blood magic (including human sacrifice; *see*

BLOOD MAGIC) into their rituals of supplication. The Temple of the Lord of Light (one of several Red Temples) is located in Volantis and is guarded by a slave army called the Fiery Hand. Adherents of this religion sometimes see fire visions. They anticipate an eschatological figure known as the "Prince (or Princess) that was Promised." This figure is expected to defeat the Great Other and his forces of cold and darkness.

RAT COOK | A rodent of unusual size. In a popular northern legend, a cook who wanted revenge on an Andal king cooked the king's son in a pie with vegetables and bacon. Because the cook killed a guest in his house, the gods turned the cook into a giant rat. The gods mandated that the former cook could only eat his own offspring. According to some stories, the Rat Cook roams the halls of the Nightfort eating his young but never dulling his hunger. This myth reinforces the religious ideal of guest right (prohibiting the murder of hosts and guests).

RAVENS | Domesticated ravens are used in Westeros as letter carriers. In the cave of Brynden "Bloodraven" Rivers, several ravens embody the impressions of Greenseer souls. Skinchangers of long ago once projected themselves into these ravens and a part of them remains within them.

RED GOD | *See* R'HLLOR.

RED PRIESTS | *See* R'HLLOR.

RED SWORD OF HEROES | A legendary weapon. This is another name for a mythical blade named "Lightbringer" wielded by Azor Ahai. *See* AZOR AHAI.

RED TEMPLE | *See* R'HLLOR.

SEPTAS | Female clerics of the Faith of the Seven. They will sometimes serve in septs (*see* SEPTS). They also serve as governesses for wealthy families.

SEPTONS | Male clerics of the Faith of the Seven. They perform ceremonies related to namedays, weddings, and general worship.

SEPTRIES | Westerosi places of isolated worship. The Faith of the Seven maintains monastic communities called septries. A septry is managed by an Elder Brother and lesser brothers called proctors. Septries tend and process agricultural products like dairy and honey. As these monastic communities are separated by gender, convent-like communities are called "motherhouses."

SEPTS | Places of worship devoted to the Seven-Faced God. They are seven-sided buildings with a depiction of an aspect of god on each wall. Most towns, cities, and great houses of Westeros feature a sept. The Great Sept of Baelor represents the hub of power for the Faith in King's Landing. Before Baelor's Great Sept was constructed, the Starry Sept at Oldtown was the seat of the High Septon.

SERPENT GOD OF LYBER | *See* SPIDER GODDESS OF LYBER

SEVEN-FACED GOD | The most venerated god in Westeros. Sometimes called the "new gods," this singular deity is represented by seven archetypal aspects: Father, Mother, Maiden, Crone, Warrior, Smith, and Stranger. Each of these aspects is prayed to depending on the concern of the person praying. The Father is venerated for justice and judgement; the Mother for mercy and fertility; the Maiden for purity and love; the Crone for wisdom and foresight; the Warrior for protection and courage; the Smith for craftsmanship. The Stranger is not often prayed to as (s)he represents death. Male clerics are called septons. The leader of the Faith is called the High Septon. Female clerics are called septas. Adherents believe in seven heavens and seven hells. *See also* SEPTS AND SEPTRIES.

SHADOWBINDERS | Magic-wielding freaks. Associated primarily with Asshai sorcery, shadowbinders have a nefarious reputation with outsiders. Many hide their eyes behind masks, attracting even more misgivings. Some believe they are hiding their eyes from the gods. Melisandre (rightly or wrongly) is sometimes called a shadowbinder. If her ability to birth a shadow assassin from her womb is any indication, shadowbinders can summon shadows capable of violence.

SHADOWCAT | A large Westerosi cat. This predatory feline is common throughout Westeros. Somewhere between the size of mountain lion and tiger, they get their name from their beautiful pelts of thick black fur featuring pale white stripes.

SHROUDED LORD | A figure of rumor and legend. Some stories about the Stone Men (*see* STONE MEN) tell that they are ruled by a figure named the Shrouded Lord. He is said to bestow a "grey kiss" that causes greyscale (a skin disease that leads to madness).

SILENT SISTERS | Westerosi clerics of ritual purity. This order vows silence and manages corpses for the Faith of the Seven.

SINGERS | *See* CHILDREN OF THE FOREST.

SKINCHANGERS | Also called beastlings, these are humans who spirit-cast themselves into the bodies of animals. In the Baratheon period,

the most notable skinchangers are Starks who share a spiritual connection with direwolves. Those who spirit-cast themselves into wolves are called wargs (The verb "warging," however, is sometimes used generically). Skinchangers have the ability to perceive the world through the senses of the animals they inhabit. The talent for "greensight" (envisioning past, future, and/or distant events) is related to skinchanging. Very few skinchangers are gifted with greensight. *See* GREENSEERS.

SNARKS | Creatures of superstition. Snarks are imaginary creatures described to children in scary stories. When coupled proverbially with "grumkins," snarks function as an exemplar for dubious folklore.

SOTHORYI | Creatures of rumor. One of the humanoid peoples of Sothoryos, this porcine folk is stronger than most humans but believed to be less intelligent. We cannot prove that they are not connected in some way to the Gamorreans of Jabba's Palace.

SPHINXES | Creatures of mythology. Statues of sphinxes are found throughout Westeros and Essos. They usually depict an amalgam of animals, most commonly the head of a human, the body of a lion, and wings. These statues are often found at important gateways that require pilgrims to pass through the pair.

SPIDER GODDESS OF LYBER | A sick and wrong god of Essos. Little is known of the myth that features the spider goddess. Legends from Lyber suggest that she battled a serpent god in an endless war. *See also* "ARACHNOPHOBIA" IN THE DIAGNOSTIC AND STATISTICAL MANUAL OF MENTAL DISORDERS, 5TH ED.

SQUISHERS | Creatures of rumor. They are spoken of in the crownlands and thought to resemble humans, but with larger heads, scaly skin, webbed digits, and sharp teeth. They eat little human boys and breed with girls. They are inappropriate on so many levels. Also, yuck.

STALLION WHO MOUNTS THE WORLD | *See Dosh Khaleen.*

STARRY SEPT | *See* SEPTS.

STONE MEN | An isolated group of contagious and mindless folk. Along the Rhoyne River near a place called the Sorrows, this skin-diseased community congregates by the Bridge of Dreams. Having contracted greyscale, their skin presents as cracked blisters resembling stone. The disease brings about madness and is highly contagious. *See also* SHROUDED LORD.

STORM GOD | *See* DROWNED GOD.

SUMMER ISLES GODS | Gods for swingers. Little is known of these gods from a Westerosi perspective. Their worshippers honor them with sexually ecstatic rituals. This happens both in temples and pillow houses. While the names of the gods are unknown, gods of love and fertility are believed to be among the pantheon.

TEMPLE OF THE GRACES | *See* GHISCARI GRACES.

TEMPLE OF THE LORD OF LIGHT | *See* R'HLLOR.

TYRION | *See* GOD OF TITS AND WINE.

TRIOS | A god so nice, they had to name him thrice. He is depicted with three heads. There are three towers dedicated to him in Braavos. The temple built in his honor is located in Tyrosh and stands next to a great statue by the same name.

TWO MOONS | *See* WARLOCKS OF QARTH.

UNICORNS | Legendary equestrian beasts. According to the Children, there is a species of endangered unicorns in the True North. *C'mon George, unicorns?*

VALYRIAN STEEL | A rare alloy. Abnormal in strength and quality, this metal features a rippled pattern (similar to Damascus steel). In the Baratheon period, it is rare and therefore prized for its value. In previous ages, it was valued for weapon and armor crafting. The process of forging Valyrian steel likely involved volcanic heat, dragon fire, sacred ritual, or a combination of these. The ability to make new Valyrian steel seems to have died with Old Valyria. *See* DOOM OF VALYRIA.

VARYS | *See* MERLING.

WALL | In the conversation for one of the finest Rock albums ever produced. This title also refers to the supernatural ice wall that separates Westeros from the True North.

WALRUS-MEN | Creatures of legend. In Lorathi legend, the makers of the ancient mazes were destroyed by strange creatures. Some legends suggest the Walrus-men are to blame. This sounds totally plausible as walruses are nautical bullies, sexually dimorphic, and look like Illinois state troopers.

WARGS | *See* SKINCHANGERS.

WARLOCKS OF QARTH | Mages of Essos. Based in the House of the Undying, these sorcerers seem to thrive in proximity to dragon magic. They drink copious amounts of shade-of-the-evening wine (with psychotropic properties). This drink shades their lips blue against otherwise pale faces. When enhanced by dragon magic, they are able to project and manipulate illusions.

WATER-WIZARDS | *See* MOTHER RHOYNE.

WEEPING WOMAN | A goddess of Essos. The City of Lys is dominated by worshippers of R'hllor. But many who are dying or who have relatives close to death pay homage to the Weeping Woman (also called the Weeping Lady of Lys). This goddess is thought to mourn on behalf of the dying. Statues dedicated to her include literal fountains that flow from her eyes.

WEIRWOOD | A supernatural species of tree in Westeros. Weirwoods are white, red-sapped, deciduous trees with red leaves. Inhabitants of the North believe these trees embody gods. Many castle gardens include weirwood groves for worship. Weirwood is renowned for being naturally resistant to rot and decay. The House of Black and White (*see* FACELESS MEN) uses weirwood for one of its doors. The High Septon (*see* HIGH SEPTON) uses this wood for his staff. *See also* HEART TREES.

WHITE WALKERS | Creatures of legend and rumor / homicidal artists. White Walkers (also called the Others) are ancient beings that function as demigods north of the Wall. They command an army of ice zombies made from the bodies of dead humans, giants, and beasts (*see also* WIGHTS). They bring Winter with them as they march south. They are opposed by the followers of R'hllor, the Night's Watch, and the Children.

WIGHTS | Mindless, murderous dead guys. A wight, according to northern lore, is a corpse reanimated by the White Walkers. They function collectively as a thrall army of ice zombies. Once reanimated, their corpses are slow to decay or do not decay at all. As they are already "dead" they are impossible to kill. But they can be stopped using fire, or weapons made of volcanic glass. Valyrian Steel might also prove useful.

WILDFIRE | *See* ALCHEMISTS.

WINGED KNIGHT | A legendary figure. Among the traditions of the Vale is the story of Ser Artys Arryn, the Andal. Artys flew on the back of a great falcon to defeat the Griffon King (alternatively spelled "Griffin" King). Upon this victory, Artys established the House of Arryn in the Vale.

WOOD DANCERS | *See* CHILDREN OF THE FOREST.

WOODS WITCHES | Isolated women of ill-repute. The label "woods witch" or simply "witch" is most often used for remotely located women who employ natural healing remedies and who possess the gift of prophecy. The term is sometimes derogatory, but not necessarily. In some cases it is also used of maegi (see maegi). Those called "witch" may or may not have some facility with the supernatural.

WOODWALKERS | Creatures of legend. A small, shy folk who resided in the woods once known as the Ifequevron Kingdom. Seemingly, they were wiped out by the Ibbenese. It is possible, however, that the Woodwalkers went deep into hiding.

WYVERNS | Creatures of rumor. Wyverns are dragonlike beasts sometimes found in Sothoryos. Lesser in strength and size, wyverns are sometimes confused for dragons.

YGG | A tree monster of legend. In Ironborn lore, the ygg was a pale-wooded demon tree that feasted upon human flesh. The Grey King is said to have felled the ygg to craft the first longship.

YI TISH MONKEY TAILS | In Yi Ti mythology, the sun hid its face in shame. The catastrophe was averted by the deeds of a woman possessing the tail of a monkey. While the story is vague, it further attests to the history of a Long Night (*see* LONG NIGHT). Certain Yi Tish merchants wear stylish monkey tail hats, perhaps paying homage to the legendary woman.

ZORSES | A black-and-white striped breed of horse from Yi Ti. By reputation, they are able to travel long distances with little provision. They have neither religious significance nor magical properties. We conclude with this entry so that we can end our glossary with a Z.

A.Ron and Anthony would like to acknowledge the people that supported the Kickstarter campaign that funded the production of this book. In a very literal sense, this book would not be possible without the following incredibly supportive and generous individuals...

Gold Dragon Tier

Adam Edrington ❀ Ann Merin ❀ Ashley Nelani Paulus
Brenna Sardar ❀ Bryan Hayward Stell ❀ Caren Pelletier
Carma A. Clark ❀ Catherine ❀ Chris Churchman
Colleen Gonzalez ❀ Dani Lipari-Mareth
Danielle Mathieson ❀ David "Kamish" Stern ❀ David Aguiar
Gregory Senger ❀ Janice O'Brien ❀ Jarrod Harleman Jenni
Tahmassebi ❀ Jennie L. Rexer, PhD ❀ Jessi Pitt
Jim Quinn ❀ Joel Tacorda ❀ Kay Bonikowsky
Kilted Viking ❀ Kimmmy Lucas ❀ Kirk and Leila S
Kris Isham ❀ KWQ ❀ Lady Jillian Walsh
Laura E. Luethe ❀ Martin Monarrez
Maximus Otto of House Forster ❀ Michael Johnston
Mike McCorkle ❀ ML Fantacone ❀ Nicholas Blau
Nikki Carrow ❀ Patrick Barnhart ❀ Richard Frette
Richard Hamm ❀ Richard Kerkhof ❀ Ser Andrew Hoover
Shawn ❀ Sir Kory of House Boogerlip ❀ Steven Sprague
Tim Satterlee ❀ Tim Wolffgang Rasmussen
Tony "letrbuck" Busby ❀ Tyler Shumway
Valerie "Best Little Sister Ever" Bedel
William Blake ❀ xulsolar22

Silver Stag Tier

A.K. Cuttner * Alex M Capasso * Alexandria Leuzzi *

Andrew Kasprisin * Andrew McLeod Maggard * Ashley Wagner

Audrey Heathman * Austin Egloff * Barksdale Hortenstine, Jr.

Blake Bequette * Brad Ward * Brian Ward * c:\ * Carmelita Valdez McKoy * Cecelia Gray *

Cecily * Chase R.R. Mulberry

Chelsea Tyus * Chris Mullan * Chris Webber * Christine Brown

Christine Shrum * Christopher Carter * Chuck James

Cody Harris * Craig Gutteridge * Dan Burns & Amanda Nicholson

Dave Milne * David K. * Dean M. Welsh * Doshy Ellison

Drew Davis * Dustin Mott * Dylan Blank * Dylan P. Angeline

Eddie & Amy Cook * Eric from Minneapolis * Eric Harzer

Erica Scharbach * Erin C. Badillo * Exilein * Georgia Leigh

Graham Conroy * Gregory Rasp * House McGee * Ivonne Reyna

J. Ayala * Jacob Bryant * Jake Ollanketo * Jamie E. Massaro

Jamie H. * Jared from KC * Jasneet Mander * Jeanette Volintine

Jeremy N. * Jernious Pennyford

Joanna - "The Winged Wolf" De Arman * Joel Johnson

Joffrey Engelman * Jon Tinter * Jord * Jordan Ellena

Jordan Nazario * Josh K. * Joshua & Katelyn Triplette

Joshua Wilson, 297th of his name * JSB * jsl * Julien

Justin Freiberg * Kate B. F. * Kevin O'Donnell * Kevin P. Cattani

Kim Cook * Kimberly L. * Kody Clark * Kyle L. Long

Lady Amanda, Mother of Cats and Dragons and defender of Boston

Laura Hamilton * Lee G. Madden * Levi & Liz * Lisa K. G.

Lord Franz Stein Master of Complaints * Lucas From Milwaukee

Lucy Feekins * Luke A. Sinden * M. Kalin-Casey

Maester Beverly Lewis * Marci McClenon * Margaret Dwyer

Marjorie Weyers * Mark Hahn * Mark P (counterpoint)

Mathew K Martinez * Maura Ruth Hashman * Meagan Ellis

Meaghan Fallano * Michael * Michael Choi * Michael James

Mike Hazen * Nate Augustine * Nathan Van Aken * Nellie Cho

Nick Z ✳ Nickolas J. Berra ✳ Nicole Whatley ✳ Olivia Deck

Patrick O'Brien ✳ Paul T. ✳ Peggy "Regular Girl" Boynton

Rachel Harrison ✳ Rev. Jeremy D. Smith ✳ Rhys Davey

Rich Glinka ✳ Robert N Costa ✳ Roger Dotsey ✳ Rosa T.

SBench2 ✳ Sean Patrick Dennison ✳ Seth Edwards

Shaun Gresham ✳ Stephen M. Reynolds ✳ Steve Heineman

Steve Lionetti ✳ Steven Duran ✳ Thomas S. Melanson

Tiffiny Mansouri ✳ Tim Grable ✳ Tom de Planque

Trevor A. Ramirez ✳ Tyler Hardy ✳ Vic Kowalski ✳ Zach Ziemke

Copper Penny Tier

Adele Beegle ∼ Alec Jenkins ∼ Alexa Sonderman ∼ alina_mac ∼ Amy Wagner
Andres Blanco ∼ Anthony Fassano Anthony Sosa ∼ Caleb Thrower ∼ Casey Caldwell
Cherri Wright ∼ Chris "Flukes" Chambers ∼ Christy Heyl
Cory Peace ∼ Damien Armstrong ∼ Dan Schnock ∼ Destonie ∼ Doctor Nick
Elizabeth Adams ∼ Elizabeth Oxer ∼ Garett "gnarzz" Guenot ∼
Georgio "Bald Targaryen" Vuolde ∼ Gina Michaelson ∼ Heather J.
Heather Malin ∼ Hero James ∼ Isabel M. ∼ Jaimie Teekell ∼ James H Park
James Morris Anderson ∼ Jenni Wright Jennifer Rodriguez ∼ Jenny Olson ∼ Kevin C.
Kristina Corona ∼ Lorien Bree Leonard-Walonen ∼ Makenzie F.
Maureen Carroll ∼ MBMom ∼ Meghan Flanigan ∼ Melody H. ∼ Michael W Murphy
Michelle Tuel ∼ Mike Condo Nancy Howell ∼ Nichole H. ∼ Nick Bonds ∼ Nick Scarci
Nicole Hackney ∼ Nicole Klope ∼ Noelle Joseph ∼ Pablo Trejo ∼ Patrick Walsh
Rachel H. ∼ Renée Margaux ∼ Robert K. Crawford ∼ Ronida Oum ∼ Sarah Larsen
Sean F. Dooley ∼ Sharon Van Der Werk ∼ Stacie Calabrese ∼ Stan Lindesmith
Steve Gentile ∼ Steve Savaille ∼ thamesgirl ∼ Tom Norgate ∼ Tom_G in WV
Tracee M. Jordan ∼ Zan Shadbolt

42812781R00106

Made in the USA
Middletown, DE
17 April 2019